C000109892

Slow Cooker

Slow Cooker

Easy and delicious recipes
for all seasons

SALLY WISE

ABC
Books

The ABC 'Wave' device is a trademark of the
Australian Broadcasting Corporation and is used
under licence by HarperCollins*Publishers* Australia.

First published in Australia in 2009
by HarperCollins*Publishers* Australia Pty Limited
ABN 36 009 913 517
harpercollins.com.au

Text copyright © Sally Wise 2009
Photographs copyright © Alice Bennett 2009

The right of Sally Wise to be identified as the author of this
work has been asserted by her in accordance with the *Copyright
Amendment (Moral Rights) Act 2000*.

This work is copyright. Apart from any use as permitted under the
Copyright Act 1968, no part may be reproduced, copied, scanned,
stored in a retrieval system, recorded, or transmitted, in any form
or by any means, without the prior written permission of the publisher.

HarperCollins*Publishers*
Level 13, 201 Elizabeth Street, Sydney, NSW 2000, Australia
Unit D, 63 Apollo Drive, Rosedale, Auckland 0632, New Zealand
A 53, Sector 57, Noida, UP, India
77–85 Fulham Palace Road, London W6 8JB, United Kingdom
2 Bloor Street East, 20th floor, Toronto, Ontario M4W 1A8, Canada
195 Broadway, New York NY 10007, USA

National Library of Australia Cataloguing-in-Publication data:

Wise, Sally.
 Slow cooker: easy and delicious recipes for all seasons / Sally Wise.
 ISBN: 978 0 7333 2788 9 (pbk.)
 Includes index.
 Casserole cookery.
641.588

Cover photography by Alice Bennett
Cover design by Jane Waterhouse
Internal design by Alicia Freile
Typeset in 11.5/15pt Centaur MT by Kirby Jones
Printed and bound in Australia by Griffin Press
70gsm Classic used by HarperCollins*Publishers* is a natural, recyclable product
made from wood grown in sustainable forests. The manufacturing processes
conform to the environmental regulations in the country of origin, Finland.

This book is dedicated to my family,
and to fellow experimenters and consumers of the contents of the
faithful crock pot over so many years.

CONTENTS

INTRODUCTION

For a time, there seemed to be a common perception that crock pots were a thing of the past, a fad that came and went in the 1970s. For those of us who were young housewives at the time, however, there was hardly a benchtop that was not adorned with a resplendent orange crock pot, put to good use in making casseroles, soups and other culinary delights for our families.

With the advent of the microwave, and with women returning in even greater numbers to the workforce, and the growth of ever-so-convenient fast food outlets, crock pots faded into the background. They were eventually relegated to the depths of our cupboards and were often to be seen sitting forlornly on garage sale tables, discarded and unappreciated. But there is now a resurgence of interest in slow cookers that is causing many of us to think once more about their advantages.

They make good economic sense. Most models available today only cost a few cents per hour to operate. They also allow for forward planning in the preparation of meals. For working families, it means that dinner can be on the table in a matter of minutes after arriving home, when often the last thing we feel like doing is preparing a meal. In this way it also saves money by removing the temptation to buy pre-prepared meals on the way home.

The slow-cooking process retains maximum nutrients, as all the delicious juices are kept in the food, and the extended cooking time results in better distribution of flavours. The cooker is very versatile in that it cooks soups, seafood, chicken and meat to perfection. Vegetables are far less likely to become mushy and unpalatable, and desserts are moist and delicious. It frees up the oven for other uses, and needs little or no tending as it cooks. In summer, the kitchen does not become overheated through using the oven and in winter the kitchen is not filled with steam from pans cooking on the stove. Food is very unlikely to burn, and if we are held up at an appointment, rarely is any harm done to the food as it slowly simmers away in our absence.

Not to be neglected is the fact that almost daily we receive a barrage of information about the dangers of eating processed and takeaway foods. We are looking more closely at the number of food additives on labels, suspecting that even if they do no harm, they certainly are not doing us a lot of good. With slow cookers, we can easily control the contents of our food, all the more important for those with food allergies or intolerances, or people on special diets. Fats need to be removed from meats and poultry before adding to the slow cooker, which is also good news for our health.

It is for all these reasons that I recently pulled my old crock pot from the depths of the cupboard, feeling a little guilty for neglecting it for so long. Alongside it were three others, purchased at garage sales on a whim, in memory of how useful my old faithful had once been, promising myself to soon go back to slow-cooking with renewed enthusiasm.

I recalled with fondness how my crock pot had been associated with markers in my life. After bringing my third baby home from hospital, I used it each day, putting a simple meal into it in the relative calm of the morning, knowing that even if the sky fell in, I could rely on having a meal on the table that night. As my children went to school, I would make soup so that when they came home in the afternoon there was always a welcoming aroma and something good and nourishing to eat. Then, when I went back into the workforce, I would spend a mere few minutes before I left preparing something in the crock pot, switching it to the Low setting, guaranteed to come home to the wonderful smell of a meal well cooked, with time to spare for a cup of tea or glass of wine before serving.

All these thoughts ran through my head as I looked at the chips in the orange paintwork and dings in the shell of my old crock pot. It surely deserved better for all its hard work, and I immediately determined to bring it back to its former usefulness. This indeed has happened, and the slow cooker once again never leaves my benchtop and is constantly in use. I now wonder how I ever did without it.

As I used the crock pots more, I developed new recipes that have led to this book coming into existence. These recipes are designed specifically for slow-cooking, made with common everyday ingredients. They show that slow-cooking does not need to be confined to mere soups and stews, and showcase the flavours that can be attained so easily in our quest for tasty and wholesome food. I hope you enjoy preparing and eating them as much as I have enjoyed putting them together.

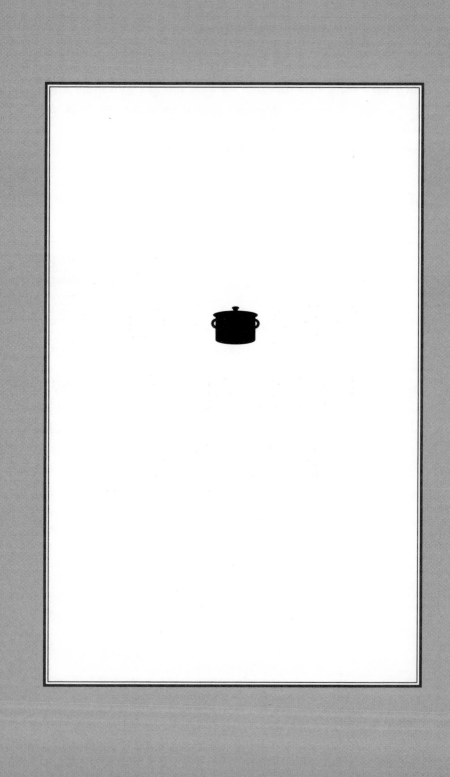

GENERAL
HELPFUL
HINTS

Recipes in this book have been prepared in a range of slow cookers, using either a 3.5- or 4.5-litre capacity cooker. Wherever the size of the cooker is crucial, this will be indicated in the recipe. Cookers with greater capacity are suitable for larger quantities and are ideal for soups and casserole style dishes to feed a crowd, or to provide enough to freeze for later use.

Some cookers, particularly the older ones, have an element at the base, whereas a number of the more current models have a side or wrap-around element. The latter are more suited to puddings, such as lemon marshmallow meringue pie.

Many slow cookers have two or more temperature settings. These settings can vary from one cooker to the next, so it is very important to read the manufacturer's instructions carefully. For instance, I have a 30-year-old cooker where 'Low' means 'Keep Warm' (by some other cookers' definitions), 'Medium' means 'Low' and 'High' means the same as other cookers.

Most modern cookers have a 'Low' and a 'High' setting. Some will have an 'Auto' option, which means it starts cooking at High, then switches automatically to Low. If a cooker has a 'Keep Warm' setting, it means that after the food is cooked it will hold the food at a safe temperature until serving time. There are also cookers which have an option to delay the start of cooking; this is not recommended for meat, fish or poultry dishes. Hence the need to read the manufacturer's instruction book to ascertain how best to utilise your slow cooker.

Size Does Matter

When purchasing a slow cooker and wondering about the right size for your needs, think about what you will be using the cooker for. A small family? Entertaining? Is one enough? (I have four slow cookers and use them all.) Also consider if you will need it to fit a cake tin, pudding basin or soufflé dish. And decide if you want one with a round or oval shape — the latter is better for cooking certain roasts, such as a leg of lamb.

Recipes in this book have been prepared using a 4.5 litre or 3.5 litre slow cooker. For any dish where size really does matter, this will be specified in the recipe instructions.

Is Slow-Cooking Safe?

Yes, slow cookers cook foods at a lower temperature for an extended period of time, but the temperatures reach a level far above the recommended food safety levels. Any bacteria are destroyed by the multi-directional heat combined with the steam created in the tightly sealed container.

Times and Temperatures

As a general rule, the Low setting is approximately 94°C (200°F) and the High setting is approximately 149°C (300°F).

One hour on High is more or less equivalent to 2 hours on Low. This may vary to a degree in some recipes, which will have instructions to this effect. Some recipes require cooking on a specific setting. For meat dishes, as a general guide only, follow the table on the next page. Check for information in the instruction book for your cooker for any variations.

Conventional recipe times	Slow Cooker – Low	Slow Cooker – High
15 to 30 minutes	4 to 7 hours	1½ to 2½ hours
35 to 50 minutes	6 to 9 hours	3 to 4 hours
50 minutes to 3 hours	8 to 16 hours	4 to 6 hours

Note: *Recipes can be cooked for one to two hours on High and then reduced to Low if this is convenient.*

For Safety's Sake

If the power goes off when you are not at home, you will unfortunately need to discard the food because the temperature may have dropped to unsafe levels, causing the food to spoil.

If you have an old cooker, you can quite easily test to see if it is cooking to temperature. Fill the cooker with 2 litres of cool water, then heat on Low for 8 hours. Remove the lid and immediately check the temperature with a food thermometer. The temperature should be about 85°C (185°F). If the temperature is lower, the cooker may not be heating effectively enough to be safe.

Always defrost foods before adding them to the slow cooker. And certainly don't use the slow cooker to defrost foods.

If you wish to prepare foods the night before to set on to cook the next morning, it is best not to put the prepared ingredients into the 'cooker insert' and then refrigerate it overnight. This is because the 'chilled insert' takes longer to come up to the required temperature in the cooker. Instead, store the ingredients in containers in the fridge (put meat and vegetables separately). It only takes a few moments to combine them in the cooker the next day. Make sure also to wipe away any food on the rim of the cooker insert after preparing ingredients in the cooker, so that a good seal forms with the lid during cooking.

When cooking foods in the cooker at altitudes over 1067 m above sea level, you will need to extend the recommended cooking time by 50 per cent.

According to food experts, food should not be reheated in the slow cooker.

It is best not to leave leftovers in the cooker as they take a long time to cool down, meaning that bacteria could potentially grow in the food during this time. Instead, place them in containers and store in the fridge or freezer. Leftovers are very tasty indeed the next day and make wonderful fillings for pies. Leftovers can be frozen for up to 3 months.

Some people recommend using an external timer for the cooker. This means that the food is placed in the cooker and set to turn on at a specific time if anyone is away from the house. Although this may be very convenient, it does carry some risks – for instance, the food left standing at room temperature may develop harmful bacteria. As a general rule, don't leave food waiting to be cooked at room temperature.

General Tips

Preheating on High may be recommended for your brand of slow cooker. Follow the manufacturer's directions in the instruction manual that comes with your cooker. If someone has donated a cooker to you minus the accompanying manual, it would be best to preheat for 20 minutes.

Always make sure not to overfill the cooker – no more than halfway to two-thirds full – otherwise the seal will not form effectively.

When lifting the lid from your cooker, lift straight up and across away from the cooker so that the moisture on the lid doesn't fall back into the food.

Oven bags can be used to line the crock insert, which will reduce washing up, although some instruction manuals carry a warning that they should not be used with chicken, lamb, pork or beef.

I have one slow cooker that is oven-safe to 160°C, which could be handy to brown toppings at times, though I don't think I'd like to put it to the test.

When adding dumplings to any dish, have ready a sheet of baking (silicone) paper slightly larger than the cooker. Spray one side with cooking oil spray or grease lightly with butter. After placing the dumplings on hot food, place the paper, greased-side down, over the cooker and replace the lid. Your dumplings are sure to be light and fluffy.

Slow cookers don't like fat, so cut fat and skin from meat and poultry before adding to the cooker.

Generally it is not necessary to stir during cooking time, so don't be tempted to lift the lid unless it is to add dumplings or other toppings, soft or thawed frozen vegetables, or dairy in the latter stages of cooking. Each time the lid is lifted, an extra 20–30 minutes must be added onto the cooking time. This is because the steam that results from slow-cooking creates a seal with the lid, and when the lid is lifted this seal is broken and needs to form again. Heat is also lost each time the lid is lifted.

If the dish is not cooked, replace the lid, set the cooker to High and cook in 30-minute increments.

Don't place the hot crock insert on a cold surface, nor a very cold crock insert into a hot unit.

Don't pour cold water into a hot crock or hot water into a cold crock.

Liquid Content

Use about half the recommended amount as you would in a conventional recipe, unless otherwise stated. If you find that the dish has too much liquid for your liking, simply turn the setting to High during the last hour of cooking.

Some books recommend taking off the lid and turning the cooker to High for a time, but I've not always found this to be successful. Instead, I take out most of the excess liquid with a soup ladle and put it into a small saucepan. I then cook it over high heat on the stovetop until it reduces right down, and then return it to the slow cooker. It only takes a few minutes and needs little attention. In this way the flavours are retained and intensified.

Another trick is to thicken this sauce in the saucepan with cornflour paste (up to 1 tablespoon of cornflour mixed to a paste with a little cold water), stirring constantly while adding, and using only as much as is needed to thicken to the desired consistency. Then return the resulting gravy to the cooker.

Many casseroles can be thickened in the cooker itself quite effectively (particularly on the High setting) by merely adding some cornflour paste, as the density and heat of the food is enough to induce the thickening in conjunction with the cornflour.

Some cookbooks advise rolling the meat for casseroles and braises in flour before adding to the slow cooker to help thicken the pan juices during cooking. I steer away from this as I have childhood memories of dinners at the house of an aunt, not a particularly good cook, whose gravies tasted like flavoured glue and had much the same consistency.

Also, by using the cornflour option (as long as maize cornflour, not wheaten cornflour, is used) the dish often can be suitable for those who are gluten intolerant.

The Flavour Factor

It is sometimes claimed that during long slow-cooking some of the flavours of the food are diminished. In fact, I have not very often found this to be the case, but I have an 'armoury' of simple products on stand-by as flavour enhancers, should they ever be necessary. It is really important to taste the food before serving (as with any form of cooking), so that flavours can be adjusted if necessary.

Although I generally refrain from using anything reeking of artificiality, I do keep on hand a top quality vegetable and/or chicken stock powder. The other items on the list of (good quality) essentials include:

soy sauce
Worcestershire sauce
sweet chilli sauce

chutney or relish
plum sauce
tomato sauce
quince or redcurrant jelly
raspberry jam
marmalade
apricot jam

You can use the commercial product or make your own (except for the soy sauce) – some easy recipes from *A Year in a Bottle* are provided at the end of this book.

Soups

Only add enough water to barely cover the ingredients and add extra water later if necessary. To make a cream soup, I make a cheese or cream sauce on the stovetop and add this at the end. This sauce can be made any time and reheated before adding to the slow cooker. Another method is to add cream or evaporated milk at the end of cooking time, replacing the lid on the cooker, turning to High and reheating for approximately 20 minutes.

Rice and Pasta

The same amount of water can be used as for conventional cooking, or reduce by one-third at most.

Rice and pasta should never be cooked for an extended period of time; 2 hours is usually ample. For pasta and rice dishes, cooked rice or pasta should be added during the last hour to half-hour of cooking time.

Seafood

When seafood is cooked in the slow cooker, it retains its shape, nutritional value and delicate flavour. When cooking a whole fish it is a good idea to line the cooker with a piece of baking paper large enough to reach up the sides, then place the fish on top. This makes lifting out the cooked fish much easier.

I have found cooking seafood highly successful in the slow cooker — it is ideal for squid, for instance, which benefits greatly from the slow-cooking process.

I have read that fish will go rubbery, mushy and unpalatable when cooked in the slow cooker. I have simply not found this to be the case, so long as it is cooked for no longer than 2–3 hours. Use the seafood recipes in this book as a guide.

Vegetables

In the slow cooker, some vegetables tend to take longer to cook than meat. Root vegetables, such as carrots, parsnips and onions, should not be cut into pieces larger than 2 cm. Place them in the base of the cooker, where they will cook faster in the simmering liquid.

Soft vegetables, such as tomatoes and zucchini, should be added in the last hour of cooking, unless you want them to break down. Frozen vegetables should be thawed and added during the last half-hour.

Dried beans should be soaked overnight, and some beans, such as red kidney beans, need to be cooked for 15 minutes and drained before adding to the cooker. Certain varieties of dried beans can be poisonous if not cooked first. If you are unsure about the type of beans you are using, it is best to cook them in this way before using in a slow cooker recipe.

I often use drained canned chickpeas or beans, and add them during the last hour to half-hour of cooking time.

Herbs and Spices

During cooking, herbs and spices may diminish in flavour. This particularly applies to dried herbs, so it is better to use fresh. I often use a combination of both. If you think the dish could do with a little more when tasting at the end of cooking time, just add extra at this point.

Be careful with adding cayenne pepper and Tabasco sauce – they can become bitter over a long period of cooking. Add them towards the end.

Dairy Products

Dairy products do not handle long periods of slow-cooking particularly well. Generally, they should be added during the last hour to half-hour of cooking.

Cheese or white sauces reputedly break down, though I have not found this to be a real issue if a combination of cornflour and eggs are added to the sauce mixture.

Low-fat cream or evaporated milk can be used instead of regular cream, and sometimes perform better than the full-fat varieties.

Meat

Cheaper cuts of meat, such as casserole steaks, are a good choice for the slow cooker, as they break down to become very tender indeed.

Some people brown meat before adding it to the cooker. Generally speaking, this is not necessary (I certainly don't bother), not even for roasts – it will just take extra time and effort and means extra cleaning up. Exceptions to this would be all kinds of minced meat, unless making a meat loaf. It only takes a few minutes to brown them – they need to be broken up anyway – and the colour and flavour of the finished dish is better.

All visible fat and gristle should be cut off meat for the slow cooker.

Roasts should be boned out for slow-cooking (ask your butcher to do this for you). Use smaller whole roasts or cut a roast beef, for example, to fit comfortably in the cooker. Any trimmings from the meat can be used later in a casserole-type dish.

Meat should be thawed before placing in the cooker. This is because foods should reach 60°C (140°F) as soon as possible, and the inclusion of frozen meat could hamper this process.

Chicken

For whole roast chicken, use a chicken no larger than 1.5 kg.

Remove skin and visible fat from chicken.

Chicken should be cooked on the High setting. You can brown the chicken in a frying pan with a little oil if you like, before adding it to the cooker, although it is not necessary to do so. A whole chicken will take about 4 hours on High to cook – its flesh will be succulent and tender.

Desserts

Slow cookers make wonderful desserts. Steamed puddings cook without filling the kitchen with steam and without needing constant attention to see if their surrounding water has run dry. It is always a good idea to preheat the cooker for a few minutes on High before adding the pudding, especially if the recipe contains self-raising flour.

Cookers with wrap-around side-elements can even be persuaded to make custard and meringue puddings very successfully on the Low setting.

Poached fruits are far more likely to keep their shape during cooking, and the colour developed with quinces over the slow-cooking time is a sight and taste that must be experienced.

Having said all this, there are a number of dessert recipes in this book which are recommended for using a specific capacity slow cooker, usually a 3.5 litre cooker. The reason for this is that the ingredient quantities better cater for a smaller size slow cooker.

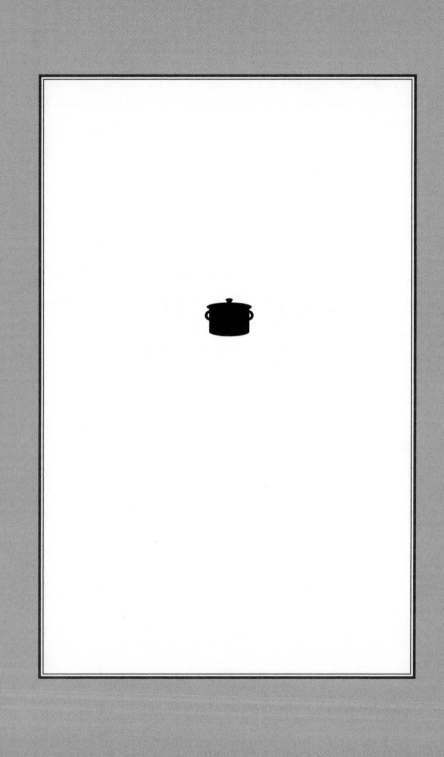

SOUPS

Pea and Ham Soup

Serves 4–6

3 carrots
½ parsnip (optional)
1 onion
300 g green split peas
300 g bacon bones or ham hock
1½ teaspoons salt
5 cups water

Peel and dice the carrots and parsnip, if using. Peel and finely dice the onion. Place in the slow cooker with the remaining ingredients and stir.

Place lid on cooker and cook for 4 hours on High or 8 hours on Low.

LEEK AND POTATO SOUP

Serves 6

1 kg leeks
600 g potatoes
2 cups chicken stock, or water with
   3 teaspoons chicken stock powder
¾ cup cream, light cream or evaporated milk
½ cup grated tasty cheese (optional)
white pepper, to taste

Remove the green section of the leeks and discard them (these would make the soup bitter). Wash the white section of the leeks well and cut into 1 cm dice. Place in the slow cooker.

Peel the potatoes and cut into 1 cm dice. Add to the cooker with the chicken stock.

Place lid on cooker and cook for 4 hours on High or 8 hours on Low.

Purée with a stick blender or in a food processor.

Turn off the heat, then add the cream and cheese, if using. Stir well to combine. Add salt and white pepper to taste. If the soup is too thick for your liking, simply thin it down with a little more cream or milk until it reaches the desired consistency.

FENNEL AND POTATO SOUP

Serves 6–8

1 kg fennel bulbs
900 g potatoes
1 small onion
100 g diced bacon
3 cups chicken stock
90 ml sour cream
2 tablespoons finely chopped mint

Remove and discard any tough sections* from the fennel and dice finely. Peel and dice the potatoes. Peel and dice the onion. Place all in the slow cooker with the bacon and stock.

Place lid on cooker and cook for 4 hours on High.

Purée or sieve until very smooth, then add the sour cream.

Serve topped with a little chopped mint.

Hint: *The tough sections of the fennel can be used later in a stock.*

MINESTRONE

Serves 6–8

2 carrots

1 onion

1 small potato

1 small zucchini

3 cloves garlic

⅓ cup chopped bacon

½ cup tomato paste

1½ cups diced fresh, canned or bottled tomatoes

2 cups water

2 teaspoons stock powder

410 g can red kidney beans, drained

1 teaspoon dried oregano

2 cups cooked small macaroni

grated parmesan, to serve

Peel and dice the carrots, onion and potato. Dice the zucchini. Peel and crush the garlic. Place in the slow cooker with the remaining ingredients, except the macaroni and parmesan, and mix well.

Place lid on cooker and cook for 4 hours on High or 7–8 hours on Low. About 30 minutes before the end of cooking time, heat the cooked macaroni and add to the cooker. Replace the lid and cook for a further 30 minutes.

Add salt and pepper to taste and serve topped with grated parmesan.

CREAM OF MUSHROOM SOUP

Serves 4

375 g mushrooms
½ small onion
1 clove garlic
¾ cup chicken stock, or water with
    2 teaspoons stock powder
½ cup cream, light cream or evaporated milk
½ teaspoon Dijon mustard (optional)

Wipe the mushrooms and slice finely. Peel the onion and garlic and dice finely. Place in the slow cooker with the stock.

Place lid on cooker and cook for 4 hours on High or 8 hours on Low.

Purée the ingredients until the desired consistency is reached. Stir through the cream. Add the mustard, if you think it is needed, and salt and freshly ground black pepper to taste.

PUMPKIN SOUP

Serves 4

750 g dark fleshed pumpkin,* such as Jap or
    Butternut pumpkin
1 onion
1½ cups stock, or water with
    3 teaspoons vegetable stock powder
½ cup cream
½ cup grated tasty cheese

Peel the pumpkin and cut into 2 cm squares. Peel and dice the onion.
Place in the slow cooker with the stock. Stir to combine.

Place lid on cooker and cook for 4 hours on High or 8 hours on Low.

At the end of cooking time, purée and stir through the cream and
grated cheese. Add salt and pepper to taste.

Hint: *Sweet potato can be substituted for the pumpkin. In this case, add the diced
flesh of half a peeled cooking apple, such as Granny Smith.*

COUNTRY CHICKEN SOUP

Serves 6

1 kg chicken drumsticks
1 onion
1 carrot
½ parsnip
60 g sweet potato
1 stalk celery
2 tablespoons green split peas
2 tablespoons pearl barley
3 cups chicken stock, or water with
    1 tablespoon chicken stock powder
white pepper, to taste

Remove as much skin from the chicken as possible. Peel and chop the onion, carrot, parsnip and sweet potato, and chop the celery. Place chicken and vegetables in the slow cooker with the split peas, barley and stock. Stir to combine.

Place lid on cooker and cook for 4 hours on High.

Add salt and white pepper to taste.

HEARTY LAMB AND VEGETABLE SOUP

Serves 6

125 g sweet potato
2 carrots
1 onion
2 lean lamb shanks
2 tablespoon green split peas
1 cup fresh, canned or frozen corn kernels
1 teaspoon salt
4 cups water

Peel and dice the sweet potato, carrots and onion. Place in the slow cooker with the remaining ingredients and stir.

Place lid on cooker and cook for 4 hours on High or 8 hours on Low.

Add salt and pepper to taste.

LEEK AND CORN CHOWDER

Serves 6

3 leeks
2 carrots
1 small sweet potato
1 small potato
6 rashers lean bacon, rind removed
1½ cups fresh, canned or frozen corn kernels
1½ cups canned creamed corn
2½ cups stock or water
1½ teaspoons salt
3–4 teaspoons cornflour
1¼ cups milk
½ cup cream
1 cup grated tasty cheese
½ teaspoon Dijon mustard

Remove and discard the green parts of the leeks. Wash the white parts carefully and dice finely. Peel and dice the carrots, sweet potato and potato. Dice the bacon. Place all the ingredients in the slow cooker with the corn, stock or water and salt. Stir to combine.

Place lid on cooker and cook for 5 hours on High or 8–9 hours on Low.

Near end of cooking time, mix the cornflour with ¼ cup of cold milk to a paste. Combine remaining milk and the cream in a saucepan and bring to the boil. Thicken with the cornflour paste, stirring to stop lumps forming. Stir in the cheese until melted. Add the mustard. Mix the cheese sauce into the chowder and add salt and pepper to taste.

POTATO AND BACON CHOWDER

Serves 8

I had read in many books that dairy does not fare well in a slow cooker, but some did mention that if light cream were used, this would work out well. So one day I decided to put this to the test by making the family favourite "Potato Bake" in my slow cooker.

I layered the potato, onion and bacon with the cream and garlic as specified, and left it to cook. However, it turned out a disaster, with lumps of cream sitting on top of a watery mass of potato, onion and bacon. Disgusted, I told my husband to feed it to the chickens the next morning. What a waste of ingredients.

As I was heading to bed, I once more caught sight of the offending dish sitting complacently on the benchtop. It suddenly occurred to me that if I blitzed it with my stick blender, there just may be a chance to retrieve it by making it into a soup.

In actual fact, it turned the mixture into a sensational creamy soup, and has since then been prepared as potato and bacon chowder with much less fuss in the making, for as a bonus I no longer need to painstakingly layer the ingredients. It is totally in keeping with our family philosophy that there is no such thing as a failure, only something we haven't found a use for yet.

1 kg potatoes (not the waxy kind)
150 g lean bacon
1 onion
2 cloves garlic
300 ml light cream
3 teaspoons stock powder
2 cups hot milk, approximately

Peel the potatoes and cut into 1 cm dice. Remove the rind from the bacon and dice. Peel and dice the onion. Place in the slow cooker.

Peel and crush the garlic and mix into the cream with the stock powder. Pour over the ingredients in the cooker.

Place lid on cooker and cook for 4 hours on High or 8 hours on Low.

Purée ingredients, adding milk until the desired consistency is reached. Add salt and pepper to taste.

Sprinkle with chopped parsley and chives to serve.

Courtney's Cream of Corn and Bacon Soup

Serves 6

1 small onion
3 rashers bacon
1 cup fresh or frozen corn kernels
400 g canned creamed corn
1 cup milk, plus 2 tablespoons extra
½ teaspoon stock powder
2 teaspoons sweet chilli sauce
2 teaspoons cornflour
90 g grated tasty cheese

Peel and finely dice the onion. Remove rind from bacon and dice finely. Place in the slow cooker with the corn kernels, creamed corn, stock powder, sweet chilli sauce and 1¼ cups of water.

Place lid on cooker and cook for 2 hours on High or 4 hours on Low.

Meanwhile, make the cheese sauce.* Mix the cornflour with the extra 2 tablespoons of milk to a paste. Place the milk in a small saucepan and bring to the boil. Thicken with the cornflour paste, then mix in the tasty cheese.

About 1 hour before the end of cooking time, mix the cheese sauce into the soup. Replace the lid and allow the soup to heat through completely on High.

Hint: *If you have any cheese sauce left over from another meal, this is a great way to use it up.*

PARSNIP AND BLUE CHEESE SOUP

Serves 4

This unusual soup is my personal favourite. Choose your audience well with this one, but it is a real treat for those who love blue cheese.

>   500 g young parsnips
>   1½ cups chicken stock
>   2 teaspoons lemon juice
>   50 g blue cheese (a hard variety, not a brie or
>   camembert)
>   ½ cup cream
>   white pepper, to taste

Peel and chop the parsnips, removing any sign of woody core. Place in the slow cooker with the chicken stock and lemon juice.

Place lid on cooker and cook for 4 hours on High or 7 hours on Low, or until the parsnip is tender.

Add the blue cheese and purée until very smooth.

Stir in the cream and add salt and a little white pepper to taste.

Note: *Reduce the amount of stock and eliminate the cream to turn this into a parsnip and blue cheese dip.*

SUBTERFUGE SOUP

Serves 6

As any parent is well aware, children can be fussy about eating vegetables. With six children in our household, there was always someone who didn't like something at some stage. For instance, our youngest, Courtney, loved broccoli, calling it 'trees' from the age of 9 months, but most of the others loathed it.

To avoid major or minor conflict at the dinner table, I invented this soup as a subtle form of subterfuge to maximise the chance of getting a range of vegetables into them. It worked really well. For instance, if the broccoli remained untouched on the main course plate, it didn't matter too much as they had unknowingly consumed it in the soup. I don't use the florets, but would peel and chop the stalk for the purpose so specks of the head of broccoli weren't evident. This saved wastage as well.

It is a really tasty soup in its own right and I still make it often. If you are feeding fussy children, just remember to be discreet. Don't use strong vegetables such as swede or turnip – they will be spotted in a moment. I often used sweet potato and pumpkin, so should I be asked if pumpkin were in the soup, I could evasively reply that the colour was from the sweet potato, which was technically correct.

Including a small piece of cooking apple also gives the soup a subtle sweetness.

1 onion
1 kg mixed fresh vegetables*
3 cups chicken or vegetable stock, or water with
   3 teaspoons stock powder
½ cup cream, light cream or evaporated milk
½ cup grated tasty cheese (optional)

Peel the onion and other vegetables and cut into 1 cm dice. Place in the slow cooker. Add the stock and mix well.

Place lid on cooker and cook for 3 hours on High or 6 hours on Low.

Purée until very smooth. Stir in the cream and cheese, if using. Add salt and pepper to taste.

Hint: *A good combination of vegetables could include pumpkin, sweet potato, a small piece of parsnip, peeled broccoli stalks, potato, carrot (which should be finely diced) and even a few celery leaves.*

PAN CROCK BREAD

Serves 4

This is a wonderful light and moist loaf of bread, which is delicious with soups. The recipe was invented quite by accident one day when a friend came to visit. Noticing a bowl of bread dough on the kitchen bench, he commented, 'And this is for the crock pot too?' Although I had not planned for it to be, I thought 'Why not?'

> 2 cups plain flour*
> 2 teaspoons dried yeast
> 1½ teaspoons sugar
> 1 teaspoon salt
> 1 tablespoon olive (or other) oil

Grease a 16-cm round cake tin with butter or spray with cooking oil. Line the base of the tin with a circular piece of baking paper to fit in place. Then grease the baking paper with butter or spray with cooking oil.

Mix the flour, yeast, sugar and salt in a bowl. Make a well in centre and add the oil and enough lukewarm water (see note) to make a soft dough. Mix well, cover with a tea towel and leave to rise until doubled. Turn out onto a lightly floured board and knead the dough briefly.

Place dough in prepared tin and set aside to rise for approximately 20 minutes, until it reaches the top of the tin.

About 15 minutes before the bread is fully risen, preheat the slow cooker on High, adding hot water to a depth of 1 cm. Place a small wire rack in the base of cooker. Once the bread has risen, place cake tin on top of rack.

Place lid on cooker and cook for 2 hours on High.

Hint: *You can substitute $^1/_2$ cup of wholemeal flour for $^1/_2$ cup of the plain flour, if you like.*

Note: *It is not possible to specify a set amount of water, as flour moisture content can vary and can also be affected by the moisture in the atmosphere. Just make sure your dough is soft so that the yeast can do its work.*

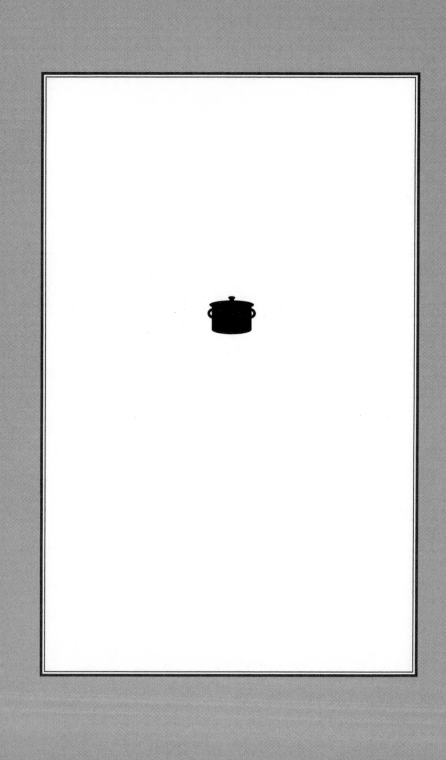

BEEF

RICH BEEF CASSEROLE

Serves 4–6

2 carrots
1 onion
½ capsicum
750 g lean diced beef
½ cup sliced mushrooms (optional)
¼ cup red wine
2 tablespoons tomato sauce (ketchup)
1 tablespoon soy sauce
2 teaspoons Worcestershire sauce
3 teaspoons chutney
1 teaspoon salt
3 teaspoons cornflour (optional)

Peel and slice the carrots. Peel and dice the onion. Remove the seeds and membrane from the capsicum and dice. Place in the slow cooker with the beef, mushrooms, if using, wine, sauces, chutney, salt and ½ cup of water.

Place lid on cooker and cook for 4 hours on High or 6 hours on Low.

If necessary, mix cornflour with ¼ cup of cold water to a paste and use a little or all of it to thicken the dish.

Add salt and pepper to taste.

POT ROAST OF BEEF

Serves 4–6

1 small onion
1 carrot
1 small parsnip
1.5 kg piece lean topside, all outer fat removed
1 teaspoon dried mixed herbs
½ cup red wine
½ cup tomato sauce
3 teaspoons cornflour

Peel and finely chop the onion. Peel and slice the carrot and parsnip.

Place the meat in the slow cooker, add the vegetables and top with the herbs, ¼ cup of water, the red wine and tomato sauce (in this order).

Place lid on cooker and cook for 4 hours on High or 8 hours on Low or until tender.

Remove the meat and vegetables from the cooker. Mix the cornflour with ¼ cup of cold water to a paste and use a little of it to thicken the gravy. Add salt and pepper to taste.

BRAISED STEAK AND MUSHROOMS

Serves 6

2 onions
600 g mushrooms
1 kg lean diced beef (chuck or blade is ideal)
1 tablespoon lemon juice
1 teaspoon salt
1 tablespoon cornflour (optional)

Peel and dice the onions. Wipe and slice the mushrooms. Add to the slow cooker with the beef, lemon juice, salt and 2 cups of water.

Place lid on cooker and cook for 4 hours on High or 8 hours on Low.

If necessary, mix the cornflour with about 2 tablespoons of cold water to a paste and use a little or all of it to thicken the mixture.

Add salt and pepper to taste.

Note: *This dish also makes an excellent filling for pies.*

STEAK AND STOUT

Serves 4

2 onions
1 clove garlic
1 cup stout
750 g lean diced beef
1½ teaspoons salt
3 teaspoons cornflour (optional)

Peel and chop the onions. Peel and crush the garlic. Place in the slow cooker with the stout, beef and salt. Stir to combine.

Place lid on cooker and cook for 5–6 hours on High.

If necessary, mix the cornflour with ¼ cup of cold water to a paste and use a little or all of it to thicken the dish. Add salt and pepper to taste.

Note: *This tasty mixture also makes a wonderful filling for a pie.*

BEEF BOURGUIGNON

Serves 6–8

1.5 kg lean stewing beef, such as chuck or blade
150 g lean rindless bacon
12 small onions
125 g mushrooms
1 teaspoon salt
1 teaspoon stock powder
¼ teaspoon dried thyme
¼ teaspoon dried marjoram
1 cup red wine
2 teaspoons tomato sauce (ketchup)
2 teaspoons Worcestershire sauce
1 tablespoon cornflour (optional)

Cut all visible fat from the beef and cut into 1.25 cm dice. Dice the bacon and peel the onions. Place all in the slow cooker and stir to combine. Wipe and slice the mushrooms and place on top.

Mix together the salt, stock powder, thyme, marjoram, red wine, tomato sauce and Worcestershire sauce and pour over contents of cooker.

Place lid on cooker and cook for 4–5 hours on High or 8–9 hours on Low.

If necessary, mix the cornflour with about 2 tablespoons of cold water to a paste and use a little or all of it to thicken the dish. Add salt and pepper to taste.

STROGANOFF

Serves 6

1 kg blade steak (or similar)
2 onions
2 cloves garlic
350 g mushrooms
3 large tablespoons tomato paste
1 tablespoon Worcestershire sauce
2 teaspoons salt
1 tablespoon cornflour (optional)
⅓ cup sour cream
hot buttered noodles, to serve

Remove any visible fat from the steak and cut into 5 cm x 8 mm strips. Peel and dice the onions. Peel and crush the garlic. Wipe and slice the mushrooms.

Place the onion and garlic in the base of the slow cooker, top with the meat, then the mushroom.

Mix together the tomato paste, Worcestershire sauce, salt and 1 cup of water and pour into the cooker.

Place lid on cooker and cook for 5 hours on High or 8 hours on Low.

If necessary, mix the cornflour with about 2 tablespoons of cold water to a paste and stir in a little or all of it to thicken the dish. Allow to cook for 5 minutes more, then mix in the sour cream. Add salt and pepper to taste. Serve with hot buttered noodles.

CORNED BEEF

Serves 6

1 onion
1 carrot
1 stalk celery
1.5 kg piece corned silverside
1 teaspoon mixed spice
8 cloves
10 peppercorns
2 tablespoons brown sugar
2 tablespoons vinegar

Peel and chop the onion. Peel the carrot and cut into chunks. Slice the celery. Place the silverside, vegetables, mixed spice, cloves, peppercorns, brown sugar and vinegar in the slow cooker.

Add enough water to come two-thirds up the silverside.

Place lid on cooker and cook for 4–5 hours on High or 8–9 hours on Low.

SWEET AND SOUR BEEF

Serves 4

3 carrots

1 onion

1 red capsicum

600 g diced beef

2 teaspoons soy sauce

2 teaspoons Worcestershire sauce

2 teaspoons chutney

½ cup brown sugar

½ cup cider vinegar

4 pineapple rings, diced,
   or 250 g canned pineapple pieces

½ cup pineapple juice

1 teaspoon salt

3 teaspoons cornflour

Peel and slice the carrots. Peel and dice the onion. Remove the stalk, seeds and membrane from the capsicum and chop into 2.5 cm pieces. Place in the slow cooker with ½ cup of water and the remaining ingredients, except the cornflour.

Place lid on cooker and cook for 4–5 hours on High or 8–9 hours on Low.

Mix the cornflour with ¼ cup of cold water to a paste and use a little or all of it to thicken the dish to the desired consistency. Add salt and pepper to taste.

GINGER AND RED PEPPER BEEF

Serves 4–6

1 large red capsicum
1 kg blade steak
1 tablespoon grated green ginger root
½ tablespoon crushed garlic
2 tablespoons tomato sauce (ketchup)
2 tablespoons plum sauce
1 tablespoon Worcestershire sauce
1 tablespoon soy sauce
2 tablespoons cider vinegar
1 tablespoon sherry
1½ teaspoons salt
1 tablespoon cornflour (optional)
steamed rice, to serve

Remove stalk, seeds and membrane from capsicum and cut into strips. Remove any visible fat from the steak and cut into strips. Place in the cooker. Add remaining ingredients, except the cornflour. Stir to combine.

Place lid on cooker and cook for 4 hours on High or 7–8 hours on Low.

If necessary, mix the cornflour with about 2 tablespoons of cold water to a paste and use a little or all of it to thicken the dish. Add salt and pepper to taste. Serve with steamed rice.

DEVILLED BEEF

Serves 4–6

1 kg gravy beef or similar
⅓ cup tomato sauce (ketchup)
2 tablespoons vinegar
1 tablespoon Worcestershire sauce
1 tablespoon brown sugar
2 teaspoons seeded mustard
2 teaspoons lemon juice
2 teaspoons sherry
1½ teaspoons salt
3 teaspoons cornflour
mashed potato and seasonal vegetables, to serve

Remove all visible fat from the beef and cut into approximately
7 cm x 4 cm pieces.

Mix together the tomato sauce, vinegar, Worcestershire sauce,
brown sugar, mustard, lemon juice, sherry and salt. Pour
3 tablespoons of the mixture over the base of the slow cooker and
place the beef on top. Pour the remaining liquid over the beef.

Place lid on cooker and cook for 4–5 hours on High or 8–9 hours
on Low.

Meanwhile, mix the cornflour with about 2 tablespoons of cold water
to a paste.

Remove the meat and pour the juices from cooker into a small
saucepan. Cook over high heat on stovetop until it has reduced to

about half its original volume. Thicken with a little or all of the cornflour paste to make a smooth gravy. Add salt and pepper to taste.

Return meat to cooker and cover with the gravy. Place lid on cooker and cook on High for a few more minutes.

Serve with creamy mashed potato and seasonal vegetables.

CARBONADE OF BEEF

Serves 4

750 g lean stewing beef, such as chuck, blade or gravy beef
2 onions
1½ cups beer
2 teaspoons Worcestershire sauce
1½ teaspoons salt
1 small French bread stick
3 teaspoons seeded mustard
¾ cup grated tasty cheese, or half grated tasty cheese
    and half grated parmesan cheese
2 teaspoons cornflour (optional)
mashed potato, to serve

Cube beef, remove any fat. Peel and finely dice the onions. Place in slow cooker with the beer, Worcestershire sauce and salt. Stir to combine.

Place lid on cooker and cook for 4–5 hours on High or 8 hours on Low.

Cut the bread stick into 2 cm slices (you need 8–10 slices). Spread each slice with mustard. Place bread slices mustard-side up on top of the beef mixture and press down into the juices. Scatter the cheese over the top. Replace lid and cook for a further 10 minutes, or until the cheese has melted.

Remove the bread slices with a slotted spoon. If necessary, mix the cornflour with 1 tablespoon of cold water to a paste and use a little or all of it to thicken the carbonade. Add salt and pepper to taste. Top each serve with two slices of the bread and creamy mashed potato.

OLD-FASHIONED BEEF CURRY

Serves 4–6

800 g lean stewing beef, such as chuck, blade
   or gravy beef
2 onions
2 carrots
½ small parsnip
2 teaspoons curry powder
1 tablespoon soy sauce
1 tablespoon Worcestershire sauce
1 tablespoon chutney
1 tablespoon apricot jam
1½ cups stock or water
1½ teaspoons salt
1 tablespoon cornflour (optional)

Trim all visible fat from the meat and dice. Peel and dice the onions.
Peel and slice the carrots and parsnip. Place in the slow cooker, along
with the curry powder, soy sauce, Worcestershire sauce, chutney,
jam, stock or water and salt. Stir well to combine.

Place lid on cooker and cook for 4–5 hours on High or 8 hours
on Low.

If necessary, mix the cornflour with about 2 tablespoons of cold
water to a paste and use a little or all of it to thicken the dish. Add
salt and pepper to taste.

TILLY'S INDIAN SWEET CURRY BEEF

Serves 6

This curry recipe came back from India with the surgeon grandfather of our elderly friend Tilly. It is ideally suited to long, slow cooking. Reduce the curry powder if you like less heat, though it is not as fiery as you might think at first glance.

2 carrots
1 onion
1 stalk celery
2 apples
1 kg lean stewing beef, such as chuck,
    gravy beef or blade
1 tablespoon sultanas
1 tablespoon relish or chutney
1 tablespoon tomato sauce (ketchup)
1 tablespoon Worcestershire sauce
1 tablespoon golden syrup
2 tablespoons brown sugar
1½ tablespoons curry powder
2 teaspoons salt
½ cup stock or water
3 teaspoons cornflour (optional)
steamed rice, to serve

Peel the carrots and onion and cut into 1 cm dice. Cut the celery into 1 cm slices. Peel, core and grate the apples. Place in the slow cooker.

Remove any visible fat from the meat and cut into 2 cm dice. Place on top of vegetables. Add the sultanas, relish or chutney, tomato sauce, Worcestershire sauce, golden syrup, brown sugar, curry powder, salt and stock or water. Stir gently to combine.

Place lid on cooker and cook for 4–5 hours on High or 8–9 hours on Low.

If necessary, mix the cornflour with about 2 tablespoons of cold water to a paste and use a little or all of it to thicken the curry. Add salt and pepper to taste. Serve with steamed rice.

BOBOTIE

Serves 4–6

2 slices white bread
1 cup milk
1 onion
2 tablespoons olive oil
750 g good quality beef mince
2 teaspoons curry powder
1 tablespoon brown sugar
1 tablespoon vinegar
1 tablespoon chutney
1 teaspoon salt
½ teaspoon finely grated lemon rind
2 eggs

Break up the bread into 2 cm squares into a bowl and pour the milk over it. Leave to stand for a few minutes.

Meanwhile, peel and dice the onion. Heat the oil and sauté the mince and onion until the mince is lightly browned. Add the curry powder and cook for a further minute. Turn down the heat, then add the sugar, vinegar, chutney, salt and lemon rind. Squeeze the bread, reserving the milk, and add to the mince mixture. Stir as you cook for a further minute. Spoon into the slow cooker.

Beat the eggs with the reserved milk and pour evenly over the mixture in the cooker.

Place lid on cooker and cook for 2 hours on High or 3 hours on Low.

OSSO BUCO

Serves 4

1 kg shin beef on the bone (about 3 pieces)
1 onion
1 carrot
1 stalk celery
2 cloves garlic
1 teaspoon dried thyme
1 sprig thyme
1 teaspoon salt
2 large tablespoons tomato paste
1 cup white wine
1½ cups diced fresh, canned or bottled tomatoes
1 tablespoon cornflour

Cut the outer fat from the meat. Peel and dice the onion. Peel and slice the carrot. Cut the celery into 1 cm slices. Peel and crush the garlic. Place all the vegetables in the slow cooker and place the meat on top.

Sprinkle over the thyme and salt. Spread the tomato paste over the top, then pour in the wine and tomato.

Place lid on cooker and cook for 5 hours on High or 8–9 hours on Low.

Mix the cornflour with about 2 tablespoons of cold water to a paste and use a little or all of it to thicken the sauce. Add salt and pepper to taste.

GOULASH WITH HERB DUMPLINGS

Serves 4–6

2 onions
3 cloves garlic
750 g lean chuck or blade beef
2 cups diced fresh, canned or bottled tomatoes
3 tablespoons tomato paste
2 tablespoons sweet paprika
2 teaspoons vegetable or beef stock powder

Herb Dumplings

2 teaspoons butter
1 cup self-raising flour
½ teaspoon salt
1½ teaspoons chopped thyme
1 tablespoon finely chopped parsley
milk, to combine

Peel and dice the onions. Peel and crush the garlic. Trim all visible fat from the meat and dice. Place the onion and garlic in the slow cooker, then put the meat on top with the tomato, tomato paste, paprika, stock powder and 1 cup of water. Mix to combine.

Place lid on cooker and cook for 4 hours on High or 8 hours on Low. Add salt and pepper to taste. Replace lid on cooker.

About 30 minutes before the end of cooking time, turn the cooker setting to High (if it has been cooking on Low), in preparation for cooking the dumplings.

To make the herb dumplings, rub the butter into the combined flour and salt with your fingertips until the mixture resembles fine breadcrumbs. Add the thyme and parsley, and mix to a soft dough with a little milk. Roll into walnut-size balls.

Remove lid from cooker. Place dumplings on top of goulash. Have ready a piece of baking paper slightly larger than the cooker and spray one side with cooking oil. Place paper greased-side down over the cooker. Place lid on top and cook for 30 minutes on High.

Steak and kidney sponge

Serves 6

300 g lamb kidneys
1 kg oyster blade steak, or similar
2 onions
1 tablespoon Worcestershire sauce
1 tablespoon chutney
2 teaspoons quince jelly*
¼ cup red wine
1¼ teaspoons salt
1 tablespoon cornflour
1¼ cups self-raising flour
¼ teaspoon mustard powder
2 eggs
1 cup milk
60 g butter, melted, plus 1 teaspoon extra

Cut the kidneys in half and remove the hard core. Cut into 1 cm dice. Remove any visible fat from the steak and cut into 2 cm dice. Peel and dice the onions. Place all in the slow cooker.

Add the Worcestershire sauce, chutney, quince jelly, wine and 1 teaspoon of salt to the cooker. Stir to combine.

Place lid on cooker and cook for 4–5 hours on High or 7–8 hours on Low, or until the meat is tender.

Mix the cornflour with about 2 tablespoons of cold water to a paste and use a little or all of it to thicken the mixture. Add salt and pepper to taste. Turn cooker setting to High and replace lid.

Place flour, mustard powder and remaining salt in a bowl and make a well in centre. Separate the eggs. Whisk the yolks and milk together until well combined and pour into the dry ingredients, along with the melted butter. Mix together with a metal spoon.

Whisk the egg whites until stiff peaks form, then fold into the flour mixture. Pour evenly over the steak and kidney mixture. Spray a piece of baking paper, slightly larger than the cooker, with cooking oil and place greased-side down over cooker.

Replace lid and cook for 45 minutes on High.

Rub over surface of the sponge with the extra butter and sprinkle with a little freshly ground black pepper.

Hint: *Redcurrant or cranberry jelly, or even plum or apricot jam can be used in place of the quince jelly.*

SAVOURY BEEF

Serves 4–6

Savoury beef makes a tasty filling for pies, large or small. To make a quick pie, I keep cooked squares or triangles of puff pastry and place them on top of hot savoury beef straight from the cooker. Leave them there for a few minutes, with the lid off, where they heat through quite rapidly. This dish also makes an excellent base for cottage pie. After cooking, spoon creamy mashed potato over the top and scatter with grated cheese. Replace the lid and leave for a few minutes in the slow cooker until the cheese has melted.

125 g lean bacon
1 onion
1 carrot
½ stalk celery
2 teaspoons olive oil
750 g good quality beef mince
1½ cups stock, or water with
    2 teaspoons stock powder
1 tablespoon tomato sauce (ketchup)
2 teaspoons Worcestershire sauce
2 teaspoons soy sauce
2 teaspoons sweet chilli sauce
¾ teaspoon salt
1 tablespoon cornflour (optional)
seasonal vegetables, to serve

Remove the rind from the bacon and chop finely. Peel the onion and carrot and chop finely, along with the celery.

Heat the oil in a heavy-based saucepan and cook the bacon and mince until brown. Transfer to the slow cooker.

Pour the stock into the saucepan and bring to the boil, stirring. Pour over the meat. Add the chopped vegetables, then the sauces and salt. Stir to combine.

Place lid on cooker and cook for 4 hours on High or 7–8 hours on Low.

If necessary, mix the cornflour with about 2 tablespoons of cold water to a paste and use a little or all of it to thicken the dish. Add a little extra salt and a little pepper if needed. Serve with seasonal vegetables.

STUFFED CAPSICUMS

Serves 4–6

For this recipe, the extra visual appeal to the dish is using different colour capsicums, if you can get them, otherwise just use three of any colour available.

    1 red capsicum
    1 green capsicum
    1 yellow capsicum
    1 onion
    1 cup fresh breadcrumbs
    600 g good quality beef mince
    1 teaspoon paprika
    2 teaspoons Worcestershire sauce
    2 teaspoons soy sauce
    3 teaspoons chutney or relish
    ½ teaspoon salt
    ¼ teaspoon dried oregano or thyme
    1 cup diced fresh, canned or bottled tomatoes
    2 tablespoons tomato paste
    1 clove garlic
    2 teaspoons sweet chilli sauce

Cut all the capsicums in half, lengthways, then remove the stalks, seeds and membrane. Set aside.

Peel and chop the onion very finely. Place onion and breadcrumbs into a bowl with the mince, paprika, Worcestershire sauce, soy sauce, chutney or relish, salt and herbs. Mix until well combined.

Mix together the diced tomato, tomato paste, garlic and sweet chilli sauce. Spread over the base of the slow cooker.

Fill the prepared capsicum halves with the mince mixture and place on top of the tomato mixture.

Place lid on cooker and cook for 4 hours on High or 8 hours on Low.

BEEF OLIVES

Serves 6

1 onion
125 g bacon
2 cups fresh breadcrumbs
¾ teaspoon dried thyme
½ teaspoon salt
1 egg
2 teaspoons sherry
1 kg barbecue steak, thinly sliced
½ small red capsicum
¾ cup diced fresh, canned or bottled tomatoes
1 tablespoon tomato sauce (ketchup)
1 tablespoon tomato paste
1 teaspoon stock powder
1 tablespoon brandy

Peel and grate the onion. Remove any rind from the bacon and dice finely. Place in a bowl with the thyme and salt. Lightly whisk the egg and add to the mixture, along with the sherry. Mix well.

Lay the meat out on a board and flatten, if necessary, with a meat hammer. Cut into approximately 10 cm x 12 cm pieces.

Divide the breadcrumb mixture between the pieces of meat and spread out over each piece. Roll up the meat and tie with butcher's string to secure filling, if you like.* Place in the slow cooker.

Remove the stalk, seeds and membrane from the capsicum. Dice finely and scatter over the meat.

Mix together the tomato, tomato sauce, tomato paste, stock powder and brandy and pour over the contents of the cooker.

Place lid on cooker and cook for 4 hours on High or 7–8 hours on Low.

Remove string from each 'olive' before serving.

Hint: *This step is a little time consuming. I generally don't do it, but just pack the 'olives' tightly together in the cooker. Inevitably this allows a little of the stuffing to escape, but still equally delicious — the gravy is just a little more textured.*

HEDGEHOGS

Serves 6

A popular dish with children. The meatballs contain long grain rice which stick out the sides of the meatballs when the rice swell with the heat and moisture of the soup, hence the name 'Hedgehogs'.

> 500 g can good quality tomato soup
> ½ cup diced canned or bottled tomatoes
> 1 large or 2 smaller onions
> 1 egg
> ½ cup fresh breadcrumbs
> 700 g good quality beef mince
> 1 tablespoon Worcestershire sauce
> 2 teaspoons soy sauce
> 3 teaspoons chutney
> 1 teaspoon salt
> ⅔ cup long grain rice

Pour the soup into the slow cooker. Add 2¼ cups of water and the tomato and stir to combine. Turn the cooker setting to High while preparing the meatballs.

Peel and grate the onion. Whisk the egg until well broken up. Combine all with the remaining ingredients. Roll into walnut-size balls and drop into the soup mixture. Make sure the liquid covers all the meatballs.

Place lid on cooker and cook for 4 hours on High or 7–8 hours on Low.

BOLOGNESE SAUCE

Serves 4–6

2 teaspoons olive oil
600 g best quality beef mince
250 g pork mince
3 onions
5 cloves garlic
1½ cups diced fresh, canned or bottled tomatoes
¾ cup tomato paste
2 teaspoons dried oregano
2 teaspoons brown sugar
1 tablespoon smooth-textured chutney
3 teaspoons Worcestershire sauce
1½ teaspoons salt
½ cup stock or water
3 teaspoons cornflour (optional)

Heat the oil in a large heavy-based saucepan. Add the beef and pork mince and cook until lightly browned, stirring every now and then to break it up.

Peel and chop the onions. Peel and crush the garlic. Add to the pan and cook for a further 2 minutes. Transfer the mince mixture to the slow cooker and add remaining ingredients, except the cornflour. Mix well.

Place lid on cooker and cook for 4 hours on High or 7 hours on Low.

If necessary, mix the cornflour with about 2 tablespoons of cold water to a paste and use a little or all of it to thicken the sauce, stirring through while still hot.

MEATBALLS WITH SPICY BARBECUE SAUCE

Serves 4

1 onion
½ stalk celery (optional)
600 g good quality beef mince
½ cup fresh breadcrumbs
1 egg
2 teaspoons soy sauce
2 teaspoons Worcestershire sauce
2 teaspoons chutney
2 teaspoons tomato sauce (ketchup)
¾ teaspoon salt

Spicy Barbecue Sauce
½ cup tomato sauce (ketchup)
1 tablespoon white or cider vinegar
2 teaspoons brown sugar
2 teaspoons honey
2 teaspoons sherry
1 tablespoon sweet chilli sauce
¼ teaspoon mustard powder

Peel and grate the onion and very finely chop the celery. Place in a bowl with rest of ingredients and mix well. Roll into walnut-size balls.

To make the spicy barbecue sauce, place all ingredients in a small saucepan and heat until the sugar is dissolved.

Cover base of the slow cooker with meatballs, leaving a little space between each. Spoon a layer of the sauce over the meatballs. Place remaining meatballs evenly over the top (there will probably only be a few extra for this). Spoon the remaining sauce over the top.

Place lid on cooker and cook for 3½–4 hours on High.

Remove the meatballs with a slotted spoon. Serve meatballs drizzled with a little of the spicy barbecue sauce.

Tomato Spiralli Beef

Serves 6

2 onions
1 red capsicum
2 cloves garlic
2 teaspoons olive oil
500 g good quality beef mince
¾ cup diced fresh, canned or bottled tomatoes
½ cup chopped semi-dried tomato
3 large tablespoons tomato paste
1 tablespoon tomato sauce (ketchup)
1 teaspoon redcurrant or quince jelly
  (even sugar will do)
½ teaspoon salt
2–3 cups cooked spiralli pasta
⅓ cup grated parmesan cheese
½ cup grated tasty cheese
green salad, to serve
garlic bread, to serve

Peel and dice the onion. Remove the stalk, seeds and membrane
from the capsicum and dice finely. Peel and crush the garlic.

Heat the oil in a frying pan and cook the mince until browned.
Transfer to the slow cooker. Add the onion, capsicum, garlic, diced
tomato, semi-dried tomato, tomato paste, tomato sauce, redcurrant
or quince jelly, salt and 1¼ cups of water. Stir to combine.

Place lid on cooker and cook for 4 hours on High or 8 hours on Low.

Heat the cooked pasta, then stir into the contents of the cooker, together with the grated parmesan. Add salt and pepper to taste.

Scatter the tasty cheese evenly over the top. Replace the lid and leave for a few minutes until the cheese melts.

Serve with green salad and garlic bread.

CHILLI CON CARNE

Serves 6

This dish is more about the flavour of the spices than the heat. However, if you would like to add some heat, try adding I teaspoon dried chilli flakes to the simmering mixture, or a fresh long red chilli or two (diced), or even a tablespoon of sweet chilli sauce.

1 tablespoon olive oil
1 kg good quality beef mince
2 onions
4 cloves garlic
2 cups diced fresh, canned or bottled tomatoes
½ cup tomato paste
1 tablespoon chutney (preferably tomato)
3 teaspoons Worcestershire sauce
2 teaspoons soy sauce
5 teaspoons ground cumin
3 teaspoons dried oregano
2 teaspoons brown sugar
1½ teaspoons salt
410 g can red kidney beans, drained
3 teaspoons cornflour (optional)
couscous, corn chips or baked jacket potatoes,
    to serve

Heat the oil in a heavy-based saucepan and cook the mince until lightly browned.

Peel and finely dice the onion. Peel and crush the garlic. Add to the saucepan and cook for a further 2 minutes. Transfer to the slow cooker. Add the tomato, tomato paste, chutney, Worcestershire sauce, soy sauce, cumin, oregano, sugar, salt and 1 cup of water.

Place lid on cooker and cook for 3½ hours on High or 6 hours on Low.

Add the beans and cook for a further 20 minutes on High. Add salt and pepper to taste.

If necessary, mix the cornflour with about 2 tablespoons of cold water to a paste and use a little or all of it to thicken the mixture, stirring it through while very hot. Cook for a further 2 minutes.

Serve with couscous, corn chips or baked jacket potatoes.

BEEF CANNELLONI

Serves 4–6

1 small onion
1 clove garlic
250 g good quality beef mince
1 cup fresh breadcrumbs
2 teaspoons plum sauce
2 teaspoons Worcestershire sauce
2 teaspoons soy sauce
60 g fetta, crumbled
1½ teaspoons salt
1 egg
2 tablespoons tomato paste
2½ cups diced canned or bottled tomatoes,
    or passata
1 teaspoon sugar
250 g instant cannelloni shells
½ cup grated tasty cheese
¼ cup freshly grated parmesan

Peel and grate the onion. Peel and crush the garlic. Add the onion and garlic to the mince and breadcrumbs, then mix together with the sauces, fetta and ½ teaspoon of salt. Whisk the egg lightly, then add to the meat and mix until very well combined.

In a separate bowl, mix together the tomato paste, tomatoes, sugar, the remaining salt and ½ cup of water. Place one-third of the tomato sauce in the base of the slow cooker.

Fill the cannelloni shells with the meat mixture.*

Put a layer of cannelloni over the tomato sauce base, then spread a small layer of the tomato sauce over it. Add another layer of cannelloni, then spread over the last of the tomato sauce on top.

Mix together the tasty cheese and parmesan and sprinkle over the top of the tomato sauce.

Place lid on cooker and cook for 2½ hours on High.

Hint: *It is much easier to fill the cannelloni shells using a piping bag. Disposable piping bags are available at most supermarkets.*

LASAGNE

Serves 6

1½ tablespoons cornflour
⅓ cup cold milk
1 egg
2½ cups milk
¼ cup grated parmesan cheese,
    plus 1 tablespoon extra
⅔ cup grated tasty cheese
5 cups Bolognese sauce (see recipe on page 76)
250 g instant lasagne sheets

To make the cheese sauce, mix the cornflour with the cold milk to a paste.

Heat the milk to boiling point and thicken with the cornflour paste. Simmer for 2 minutes, stirring constantly, then whisk in the egg. Stir through the parmesan and half the tasty cheese. Add salt and white pepper to taste.

Spread one-third of the Bolognese sauce over the base of the cooker and cover with one-third of lasagne sheets, broken into pieces to fit. Top with half of remaining Bolognese sauce, then one-third of cheese sauce and half of remaining lasagne sheets, then repeat these layers. Finish with a layer of cheese sauce.

Combine the extra parmesan and remaining tasty cheese and sprinkle over the top.

Place lid on cooker and cook for 3 hours on Low.

Braised Beef with Caraway Pumpkin Dumplings

Serves 6

800 g–1 kg stewing beef, such as chuck, blade
   or gravy beef
2 onions
1 clove garlic
1 tablespoon tomato sauce (ketchup)
2 teaspoons soy sauce
2 teaspoons Worcestershire sauce
1½ tablespoons plum or apricot jam
1 teaspoon salt
½ cup stock or water
3 teaspoons cornflour

Caraway Pumpkin Dumplings

1 cup self-raising flour
½ teaspoon baking powder
½ teaspoon salt
3 teaspoons butter
1 teaspoon caraway seeds
½ cup mashed pumpkin
1 teaspoon lemon juice
1 tablespoon milk

Remove any visible fat from the meat and cut into 2 cm dice. Peel and chop the onions. Peel and crush the garlic. Place all in the slow cooker with the tomato sauce, soy sauce, Worcestershire sauce, jam, salt and stock or water.

Place lid on cooker and cook for 4–5 hours on High, or until meat is tender.

Mix the cornflour with about 2 tablespoons of cold water to a paste, and use a little or all of it to thicken the mixture. Add salt and pepper to taste, then replace lid.

To make the caraway pumpkin dumplings, mix the flour with the baking powder and salt, then rub in the butter with your fingertips until the mixture resembles fine breadcrumbs. Mix in the caraway seeds. Make a well in the centre and add the pumpkin, lemon juice and enough of the milk to make a soft dough. Place tablespoonfuls of dough on top of the simmering beef.

Take a piece of baking paper slightly larger than the cooker and spray one side with cooking oil or grease with butter. Place the paper greased-side down over the cooker and replace the lid. Cook for 45 minutes on High.

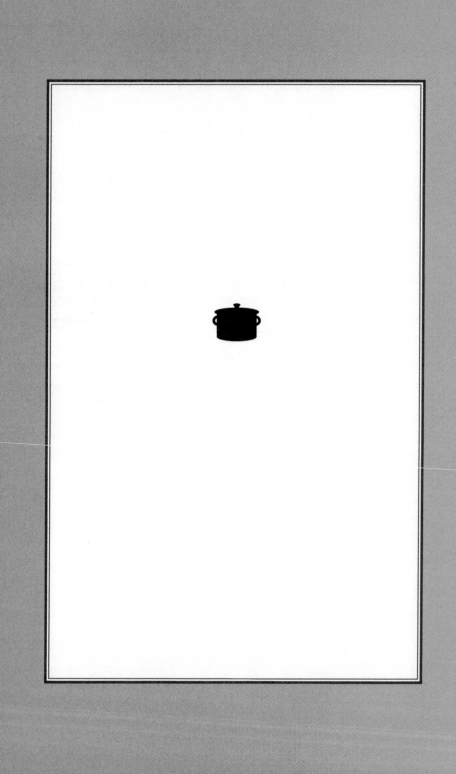

LAMB

IRISH STEW

Serves 4

The first time I made this in the slow cooker, our Irish friend Mervyn happened to come to visit us. After an ample serving of the stew, he said, 'It tastes like it came straight from my Aunt Connie's stew pot, but I'm so blootered I'll have to have a pan crock!' Little did he know the aptness of his words, prepared as the stew was in the crockpot. Translated it means: 'I'm so full I'll need to have a little lie down.'

700 g potatoes
2 onions
500 g lean diced lamb
1 teaspoon salt
3 teaspoons cornflour (optional)

Peel the potatoes and cut into 3 cm chunks. Peel and dice the onion. Place in the slow cooker. Place the lamb on top. Sprinkle with the salt and pour ¾ cup of water over the mixture.

Place lid on cooker and cook for 5 hours on High or 8–9 hours on Low.

If necessary, mix the cornflour with about 2 tablespoons of cold water to a paste and use a little or all of it to thicken the stew. Add salt and pepper to taste.

LAMB WITH APRICOTS AND ROSEMARY

Serves 6

1 onion
½ red capsicum
½ cup semi-dried tomatoes
½ cup sliced dried apricots
¼ cup chopped chorizo sausage
2 teaspoons quince or redcurrant jelly or apricot jam
2 teaspoons Worcestershire sauce
2 teaspoons soy sauce
1 tablespoon tomato paste
1 cup stock
750 g lean diced lamb
1 tablespoon chopped rosemary
2 teaspoons salt
2 teaspoons cornflour (optional)

Peel and dice the onion. Remove the stalk, seeds and membrane from the capsicum and dice. Chop the semi-dried tomatoes. Place in the slow cooker with the dried apricots, chorizo, jelly, Worcestershire sauce, soy sauce, tomato paste, stock, lamb, rosemary and salt. Stir well to combine.

Place lid on cooker and cook for 4–5 hours on High or 7–8 hours on Low.

If necessary, mix the cornflour with about 1 tablespoon of cold water to a paste and use a little or all of it to thicken the dish. Add salt and pepper to taste.

LAMB AND QUINCE HOTPOT

Serves 6

800 g lean lamb
800 g quinces
2 onions
½ cup apple juice
½ cup water
1 tablespoon Worcestershire sauce
1 tablespoon sweet chilli sauce
1 tablespoon well-flavoured chutney,
    such as green tomato
2 teaspoons tomato paste
1 teaspoon ground cumin
1 teaspoon salt
3 teaspoons cornflour (optional)

Remove any visible fat from the lamb and dice. Peel and core the quinces and cut into 1.25 cm dice. Peel and finely dice the onion. Place all in the cooker.

Add the remaining ingredients, except the cornflour, and stir to combine.

Place lid on cooker and cook for 3½ hours on High or 7 hours on Low.

If necessary, mix the cornflour with about 2 tablespoons of cold water to a paste and use a little or all of it to thicken the dish. Add salt and pepper to taste.

MIDDLE EASTERN LAMB STEW

Serves 4

This dish, with its pungent citrus and spice undertones, should be served with couscous or steamed rice and most definitely accompanied by a side dish of a little natural yoghurt sprinkled with chopped mint. To lighten the flavours a little, half a cup of natural yoghurt can also be mixed in at the end of cooking time.

750 g lean lamb
1 onion
2 cloves garlic
1 tablespoon honey
1 teaspoon turmeric
1 teaspoon ground cumin
½ teaspoon ground coriander
½ cup stock
1 teaspoon salt
1 teaspoon grated green ginger root
1 teaspoon orange rind
juice of 1 lemon
1 teaspoon brown sugar
1 teaspoon very finely diced preserved lemon rind
2 teaspoons cornflour (optional)
1 cup natural yoghurt, to serve,
    plus ½ cup extra (optional)
3 teaspoons finely chopped mint

Remove any visible fat from the lamb and dice. Peel and dice the onion. Peel and crush the garlic. Place all in the slow cooker and add the honey, turmeric, cumin, coriander, stock, salt, ginger, orange rind, lemon juice, brown sugar and preserved lemon rind and stir to mix well.

Place lid on cooker and cook for 3½–4 hours on High or 7–8 hours on Low.

If necessary, mix the cornflour with about 1 tablespoon of cold water to a paste and use a little or all of it to thicken the stew. Stir in the extra yoghurt, if desired. Add salt and pepper to taste.

Serve with the yoghurt sprinkled with the chopped mint to the side.

Lamb and Sweet Potato with Spinach and Cheesy Rice Crust

Serves 6–8

600 g sweet potatoes
1 onion
1 kg lean lamb
2 teaspoons redcurrant jelly
juice of 1 lemon
½ cup stock or water
1½ teaspoons salt
1 tablespoon tomato sauce (ketchup)
3 teaspoons sweet chilli sauce
1 tablespoon cornflour

Spinach and Cheesy Rice Crust
1 cup cold cooked rice
1½ cups self-raising flour
½ cup milk
2 eggs
2 teaspoons Worcestershire sauce
60 g butter, melted
1 cup shredded spinach or silverbeet
1 tablespoon chopped parsley
¾ cup grated tasty cheese
1 teaspoon salt

Peel the sweet potato and cut into 1 cm dice. Peel and dice the onion. Remove any visible fat from the lamb and dice. Place in the slow cooker with the redcurrant jelly, lemon juice, stock or water, salt, tomato sauce and sweet chilli sauce. Stir to combine.

Place lid on cooker and cook for 4–5 hours on High or 8–9 hours on Low.

Mix the cornflour with about 2 tablespoons of cold water to a paste and use a little or all of it to thicken the mixture. Add salt and pepper to taste. Replace lid and turn cooker setting to High.

To make the spinach and cheesy rice crust, place the rice, flour and milk in a bowl but do not stir. Separate the eggs. Whisk the egg yolks and add to the rice mixture, then add the Worcestershire sauce and melted butter and mix together very well. Add the spinach or silverbeet, parsley, cheese and salt. Mix well.

Whisk the eggwhites until stiff peaks form, then fold into the rice mixture until well combined.

Spoon the rice mixture evenly over the lamb mixture.

Replace lid and cook for 1 hour on High.

Braised Lamb Shanks with Lemon Couscous

Serves 4

3 carrots
1 onion
1.5 kg lamb shanks (4 or 5)
1 clove garlic
250 g tomatoes, chopped
1 cup tomato sauce (ketchup)
½ cup medium dry or dry sherry
1 heaped tablespoon tomato paste
2 teaspoons chutney
2 teaspoons quince jelly (optional)
2 teaspoons vegetable stock powder
1 teaspoon preserved lemon or grated lemon rind
1 tablespoon cornflour (optional)

Lemon Couscous
1 cup couscous
1 teaspoon grated lemon rind
½ teaspoon vegetable stock powder
1 cup boiling water
1½ tablespoons chopped parsley

Peel the carrots and cut into quarters. Peel and dice the onion. Place in the slow cooker and put the lamb shanks on top.

Peel and crush the garlic and add to the cooker with the remaining ingredients, except the cornflour, adding 1 cup of water last. Stir gently.

Place lid on cooker and cook for 4 hours on High or 8–9 hours on Low.

Add salt and pepper to taste. If necessary, mix the cornflour with about ¼ cup of cold water to a paste and use a little or all of it to thicken the pan juices. Stir through the braise and cook for a further 5 minutes.

To make the lemon couscous, combine the couscous, lemon rind and stock powder in a bowl. Pour the boiling water evenly over the couscous mixture. Cover and leave to stand for 5 minutes. Fluff up the couscous with a fork.

To serve, fold the parsley through the couscous, or sprinkle over the dish.

APRICOT AND ROSEMARY LAMB WITH REDCURRANT JUS

Serves 6

1.5–2 kg leg of lamb, tunnel-boned (see note)
1 onion
⅓ cup dried apricots
1 cup fresh breadcrumbs
2 teaspoons chutney
2 teaspoons chopped fresh rosemary leaves
½ teaspoon dried rosemary
½ teaspoon grated lemon rind
½ teaspoon salt
2 teaspoons oil (optional)

Redcurrant Jus
2 teaspoons redcurrant jelly
2 teaspoons tomato paste
1 teaspoon chicken or vegetable stock powder
2 teaspoons cornflour (optional)

Remove any visible fat from the leg of lamb. Peel and grate the onion. Chop the dried apricots. Place in a bowl with the breadcrumbs, chutney, fresh and dried rosemary, lemon rind and salt. Mix well, then stuff into the cavity of the lamb leg.

If you wish, heat oil in a heavy-based frying pan and brown the lamb lightly on all sides, before placing in the slow cooker.

Place lid on cooker and cook for 4 hours on High or 8 hours on Low.

Remove the lamb from the cooker, reserving the juices, and place on a board. Cover with foil and leave to rest while making the redcurrant jus.

To make the jus, place a strainer over a medium saucepan and strain the juices from the cooker. Add the redcurrant jelly, tomato paste and stock powder and bring to the boil. Boil until there is approximately 1 cup of liquid remaining.

If necessary, mix the cornflour with 1 tablespoon of cold water to a paste and use a little or all of it to thicken the jus. Add salt and pepper to taste.

Note: *Ask your butcher to remove the bone from the lamb for you.*

MOROCCAN LAMB

Serves 4

2 tablespoons olive oil
500 g lamb mince
1 large or 2 small onions
4 cloves garlic
2 teaspoons ground cumin
2 teaspoons ground coriander
¼ teaspoon ground cardamom
1 tablespoon chopped dried apricots
1½ tablespoons chopped dried figs
2 tablespoons slivered almonds
2 teaspoons lemon juice
1 cup stock or water
2 teaspoons honey
2 teaspoons chutney
1 teaspoon salt
1 tablespoon sweet chilli sauce
2 tablespoons chopped parsley
2 teaspoons cornflour (optional)
couscous, to serve

Heat the oil in a heavy-based saucepan and lightly brown the lamb
mince, stirring from time to time to break it up. Peel and dice the
onion. Peel and crush the garlic. Add to the mince and cook for a
further minute. Add the cumin, coriander and cardamom and cook for
another minute.

Add the apricot, fig, almonds, lemon juice, stock or water, honey, chutney, salt and sweet chilli sauce. Stir to combine. Pour mixture into the slow cooker.

Place lid on cooker and cook for 2 hours on High or 3½ hours on Low.

If necessary, mix the cornflour with about 1 tablespoon of cold water to a paste and use it to thicken the dish. Add salt and pepper to taste.

Mix the parsley through the lamb at the end of cooking time. Serve with couscous.

MOUSSAKA

Serves 6

600 g eggplants
2 teaspoons olive oil
600 g lean lamb mince
1 large onion
4 cloves garlic
2 teaspoons Worcestershire sauce
2 teaspoons chutney
1 teaspoon salt
2 large tablespoons tomato paste
1½ cups diced fresh, canned or bottled tomatoes
1 tablespoon cornflour
⅔ cup grated tasty cheese, plus ½ cup extra
½ cup grated parmesan cheese

Cheese Sauce
1½ tablespoons cornflour
2⅓ cups milk
1 egg
½ cup grated tasty cheese

Remove the ends from the eggplants and cut into 1 cm slices. Cook in two batches in the microwave for about 5–6 minutes on High. Dry on paper towel to soak up any excess liquid. Press lightly to make sure the eggplant is as dry as possible.

Heat the oil in a saucepan and brown the lamb mince, stirring from time to time to break it up well.

Peel and finely dice the onion. Peel and crush the garlic. Add to the lamb and cook for a further minute. Add the Worcestershire sauce, chutney, salt, tomato paste, tomato and ½ cup of water. Bring to the boil and cook for about 4 minutes. Mix the cornflour with about 2 tablespoons of cold water to a paste and use it to thicken the mixture.

To make the cheese sauce, mix the cornflour with ⅓ cup of the milk to a paste. Heat the remaining milk to boiling point and thicken with the cornflour paste, stirring constantly with a wire whisk. Remove from the heat and whisk in the egg and cheese.

Spray the slow cooker with cooking oil. Spread a little of the lamb mixture over the base, then add a layer of eggplant slices. Top with half the remaining lamb, ⅓ cup tasty cheese and half the remaining eggplant. Finish with the remaining lamb, ⅓ cup tasty cheese and the remaining eggplant. Pour over the cheese sauce. Scatter over the parmesan combined with the extra tasty cheese.

Place lid on cooker and cook for 2 hours on Low. Leave to stand for 30 minutes, if possible, before serving.

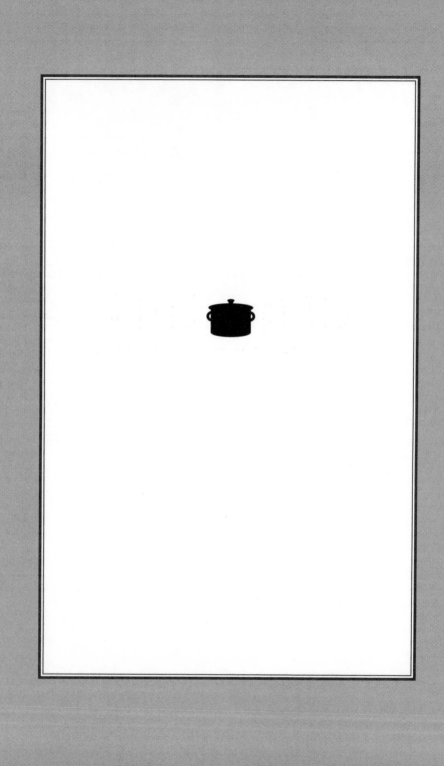

CHICKEN

CHICKEN PAPRIKA

Serves 4

1 teaspoon butter
1 tablespoon paprika
3 teaspoons sugar
2 teaspoons salt
½ teaspoon ground oregano
½ teaspoon mustard powder
¼ teaspoon ground black pepper
900 g–1 kg chicken breast fillets, skin removed
mashed potato, to serve

Grease the inside of the slow cooker with the butter.

Combine the paprika, sugar, salt, oregano, mustard and pepper in a bowl. Cut each chicken breast in two, lengthways, and coat with the paprika mixture. Place chicken in the slow cooker.

Place lid on cooker and cook for 2 hours on High.

Serve chicken with creamy mashed potato, drizzled with a little of the juices left in the cooker.

CHICKEN AND ALMONDS

Serves 6

1 kg skinless chicken breast or thigh fillets
250 g mushrooms
1 onion
2 cloves garlic
3 tablespoons slivered almonds
1 teaspoon salt
1 teaspoon chicken stock powder (optional)
3 teaspoons dijon mustard
¼ cup sherry
3 teaspoons cornflour (optional)
½ cup sour cream
¼ cup cream

Remove any visible fat from the chicken and cut into 1 cm dice. Place in the slow cooker.

Wipe and slice the mushrooms. Peel and slice the onion. Peel and crush the garlic. Place in the cooker with the almonds, salt, stock powder, if using, mustard, sherry and ¼ cup of water. Stir to combine.

Place lid on cooker and cook for 3 hours on High.

If necessary, mix the cornflour with about 2 tablespoons of cold water to a paste and use a little or all of it to thicken the dish. Add salt and pepper to taste. Stir in the sour cream and cream.

MEDITERRANEAN CHICKEN

Serves 4–6

1 kg chicken fillets (thighs, breasts or maryland)
1 onion
1 capsicum
1 cup diced fresh, canned or bottled tomatoes
½ cup tomato paste
2 teaspoons quince jelly or sugar
2 teaspoons salt
1 chorizo sausage
¾ cup pitted kalamata olives
3 teaspoons cornflour (optional)

Remove any visible fat from the chicken fillets and cut into 3 cm pieces. Peel the onion and cut into 1 cm pieces. Remove the stalk, seeds and membrane from the capsicum and chop.

Place the chicken, onion and capsicum in the slow cooker with the tomato, tomato paste, quince jelly or sugar, salt and ½ cup of water. Mix well.

Place lid on cooker and cook for 3 hours on High.

Cut the chorizo into 1 cm slices. Add to the cooker with the olives and stir. Replace lid and cook for a further 30 minutes.

If necessary, mix the cornflour with about 2 tablespoons of cold water to a paste and use a little or all of it to thicken the dish. Add salt and pepper to taste.

SATAY CHICKEN

Serves 4–6

1 kg chicken breast or thigh fillets
2 cloves garlic
2 heaped tablespoons peanut butter
5 teaspoons soy sauce
1 tablespoon Worcestershire sauce
1 tablespoon tomato sauce (ketchup)
1 tablespoon sweet chilli sauce
¾ cup coconut milk
3 teaspoons cornflour (optional)
steamed rice and seasonal vegetables,* to serve

Remove any visible fat from the chicken and cut into strips. Peel and crush the garlic. Place in the slow cooker with the peanut butter, soy sauce, Worcestershire sauce, tomato sauce, sweet chilli sauce and coconut milk. Stir to combine.

Place lid on cooker and cook for 3 hours on High.

If necessary, mix the cornflour with about 2 tablespoons of cold water to a paste and use a little or all of it to thicken the dish. Add salt and pepper to taste.

Serve with steamed rice and seasonal vegetables.

Hint: *Vegetables can be included in the sauce. Peel and finely slice vegetables such as carrot, celery and onion.*

CHICKEN WITH APRICOTS

Serves 4–6

14 canned or bottled apricot halves
1 onion
1 clove garlic
800 g skinless chicken breast fillets
½ teaspoon grated green ginger root
2 teaspoons chicken or vegetable stock powder
1 teaspoon soy sauce
2 teaspoons lemon juice
1 teaspoon brown sugar
½ cup apricot nectar
½ teaspoon salt
3 teaspoons cornflour (optional)

Place apricot halves in base of the slow cooker.

Peel and finely dice the onion. Peel and crush the garlic. Cut each chicken fillet into four pieces. Place all on top of the apricot.

Mix together the ginger, stock powder, soy sauce, lemon juice, brown sugar, apricot nectar and salt. Pour over the chicken, then stir gently to combine all ingredients.

Place lid on cooker and cook for 3 hours on High.

If necessary, mix the cornflour with about 2 tablespoons of cold water to a paste and use a little or all of it to thicken the dish. Add salt and pepper to taste.

CITRUS CHICKEN

Serves 4–6

900 g skinless chicken breast or thigh fillets
1 teaspoon finely grated orange rind
1 teaspoon finely grated lemon rind
juice of 1 orange
¼ cup white wine
1 teaspoon apricot jam (or similar)
2 teaspoons quince jelly
1 teaspoon stock powder
1 teaspoon mild-flavoured honey
½ teaspoon salt (optional)
3 teaspoons cornflour
3 teaspoons sour cream

Remove any visible fat from the chicken and cut into 10 cm x 5 cm pieces. Place in the slow cooker. Mix together the orange and lemon rind, orange juice, white wine, apricot jam, quince jelly, stock powder, honey and salt, if using. Pour over the chicken and stir to combine.

Place lid on cooker and cook for 3 hours on High.

Mix the cornflour with about 2 tablespoons of cold water to a paste and stir through the mixture. Add salt and pepper to taste.

Replace lid, turn cooker setting to High and cook for a further 10 minutes.

Stir through the sour cream just before serving.

BEDEVILLED CHICKEN

Serves 4–6

1 kg skinless chicken fillets
1 tablespoon tomato sauce (ketchup)
1 tablespoon plum sauce
1 tablespoon sweet chilli sauce
1 tablespoon lemon juice
2 teaspoons Worcestershire sauce
2 teaspoons chutney
2 teaspoons brown sugar
1 teaspoon mustard powder
1 teaspoon salt
2 teaspoons cornflour (optional)

Cut chicken into 4 cm pieces. Place in the slow cooker. Combine the remaining ingredients, except cornflour, and pour over the chicken.

Place lid on cooker and cook for 3 hours on High.

If necessary, mix the cornflour with about 1 tablespoon of cold water to a paste and use a little or all of it to thicken the dish. Add salt and pepper to taste.

THYME CHICKEN WITH APRICOT JUS

Serves 4–6

1 cup breadcrumbs

1 small onion

90 g diced bacon

1 tablespoon finely chopped pine nuts

1 tablespoon chopped lemon thyme
   or ordinary thyme

½ teaspoon dried thyme

1 egg, lightly whisked

½ teaspoon salt

1 kg chicken maryland fillets

1 cup apricot nectar or purée

1 teaspoon sugar (optional)

2 teaspoons cornflour (optional)

Place the breadcrumbs in a bowl. Peel and grate or very finely dice the onion and add to breadcrumbs with the bacon, pine nuts, fresh and dried thyme, egg and salt. Mix very well.

Open out the chicken fillets, remove any fat, and divide the mixture between them. Spread down the centre of each fillet and roll up to enclose filling. Tie each parcel with cooking string.*

Pour half the apricot nectar or purée into the base of the slow cooker and place the chicken parcels on top, packed tightly together. Spread the remaining apricot nectar over the top.

Place lid on cooker and cook for 4 hours on High.

Remove chicken from cooker and leave to rest in a dish. Remove the string from the chicken.

Add sugar to apricot mixture, if needed, and add salt and pepper to taste. If necessary, mix the cornflour with about 1½ tablespoons of cold water to a paste and use a little or all of it to thicken the jus. Serve with the chicken.

Hint: *Tying them is not really necessary, as long as the parcels are packed tightly together. However, the stuffing is guaranteed not to escape if they are tied securely.*

LEMON ROAST CHICKEN

Serves 4–6

1.5 kg chicken
2 teaspoons oil (optional)
2 teaspoons butter (optional)
1 small onion
2 large sprigs rosemary
1 lemon
¼ cup chicken stock
8 raisins
2 teaspoons redcurrant or quince jelly
3 teaspoons cornflour (optional)

Remove the skin from the chicken (don't worry about the wings, it's too difficult).

If you wish, heat the oil and butter in a frying pan and brown the chicken, turning once, before placing in the slow cooker.

Peel the onion and cut into quarters. Push into the cavity of the chicken, together with the rosemary.

Juice the lemon, retaining the rind. Pour the juice over the chicken. Cut a quarter-piece rind and place it inside the chicken.

Pour the chicken stock around the base of the chicken (not over the top) and add the raisins.

Place lid on cooker and cook for 3½–4 hours on High.

Remove chicken from cooker, retaining the juices, and leave to rest.

To make the lemon jus, strain the juices from the cooker into a small saucepan. Bring to the boil, add the redcurrant or quince jelly and reduce to about two-thirds its original volume.

If necessary, mix the cornflour with about 2 tablespoons of cold water to a paste and use a little or all of it to thicken the jus. Add salt and pepper to taste.

SPICY ROAST CHICKEN

Serves 4–6

1 chicken (up to 1.5 kg)
1 tablespoon sweet paprika
1 teaspoon ground cumin
1 teaspoon ground ginger
¾ teaspoon ground coriander
½ teaspoon stock powder or salt
½ teaspoon ground cinnamon
½ teaspoon dried mint
½ teaspoon sugar
¼ teaspoon mustard powder
¼ cup chicken stock
2 teaspoons sweet chilli sauce
1 teaspoon cornflour (optional)

Remove the skin from the chicken (don't worry about the wings, it's too difficult). Wash it inside and out and pat dry.

Combine the paprika, cumin, ginger, coriander, stock powder or salt, cinnamon, mint, sugar and mustard powder. Rub spice mixture into the surface of the chicken.

Place chicken in the slow cooker. Carefully pour the stock around the base of the chicken (not over it).

Place lid on cooker and cook for 3½–4 hours on High.

Spoon a little of the cooking juices over the chicken. Remove chicken from cooker.

Add the sweet chilli sauce to the remaining cooking juices. If necessary, mix the cornflour with about 1 tablespoon of cold water to a paste and use a little or all of it to thicken the sauce. Add salt to taste. Serve portions of chicken drizzled with a little of the sauce.

CHICKEN WITH FENNEL AND LEMON SAUCE

Serves 4–6

½ cup chopped capsicum
½ cup chopped fennel, plus sprigs to garnish
½ cup chopped semi-dried tomato
juice of 1 lemon
½ cup white wine
1 kg skinless chicken maryland fillets
2 teaspoons tomato paste
2 teaspoons quince or cranberry jelly
1 teaspoon chicken stock powder
2 teaspoons cornflour

Stuffing
1 large onion
1 small clove garlic
1 cup basil leaves
¾ cup semi-dried tomatoes
½ cup chopped red, yellow or green capsicum
1½ cups fresh breadcrumbs
½ teaspoon salt
2 teaspoons finely grated lemon rind
1 tablespoon lemon juice
1 egg, lightly beaten

Combine the capsicum, fennel and semi-dried tomato and place in the base of the slow cooker. Pour over the lemon juice and white wine.

To make the stuffing, peel and very finely dice or grate the onion. Peel and crush the garlic. Shred the basil and chop the semi-dried tomatoes. Combine with the remaining stuffing ingredients. Taste to see if more salt is needed.

Open the chicken fillets out on a board and remove any visible fat. Divide the stuffing between them, placing it along the centre of each and rolling the sides around to enclose the filling. Place the chicken fillets in the slow cooker, packed together tightly.

Place lid on cooker and cook for 4 hours on High.

Remove the chicken from the cooker and place in a serving dish.

Place a sieve over a medium saucepan and strain the juices from the cooker. Place the pan over medium heat on the stovetop and bring the juices to the boil. Add the tomato paste, quince or redcurrant jelly and stock powder. Bring to the boil and reduce to two-thirds of its original volume.

Mix the cornflour with about 2 tablespoons of cold water to a paste and use a little or all of it to thicken the sauce to a coating consistency. Add salt and pepper to taste.

Pour the fennel and lemon sauce over the chicken. Garnish with fennel sprigs.

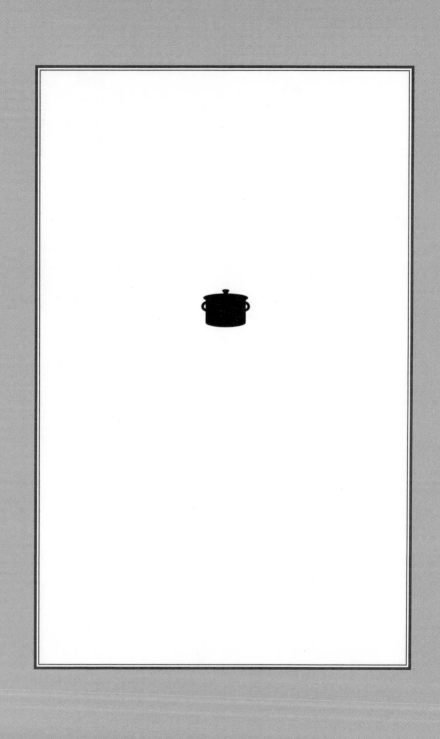

PORK

PORK IN SPICY VEGETABLE SAUCE

Serves 4–6

1 onion
1 red capsicum
400 g sweet potato
1 carrot
1 small parsnip
2 cloves garlic
1 small apple
750 g lean diced pork
¼ cup tomato sauce (ketchup)
1 tablespoon cider vinegar
2 tablespoons Worcestershire sauce
1 tablespoon brown sugar
1 teaspoon ground ginger
¼ teaspoon ground allspice
1 tablespoon cornflour (optional)

Peel the onion and dice finely. Remove the stalk, seeds and membrane from the capsicum and dice. Peel the sweet potato, carrot and parsnip and cut into 1 cm dice. Peel and crush the garlic. Peel, core and finely dice the apple. Remove all visible fat from the pork. Place all in the slow cooker with the tomato sauce, vinegar, Worcestershire sauce, sugar, ginger and allspice.

Place lid on cooker and cook for 4–5 hours on High or 7–8 hours on Low. If necessary, mix the cornflour with about 2 tablespoons of cold water to a paste and use a little or all of it to thicken the dish. Add salt and pepper to taste.

CURRIED SAUSAGES

Serves 6

2 onions

1 carrot

1 stalk celery

1 small zucchini (optional)

700 g cooked sausages

½ cup diced fresh, canned or bottled tomato

2 teaspoons soy sauce

2 teaspoons tomato sauce (ketchup)

2 teaspoons plum jam (or similar, but avoid
     jams with pips)

2 teaspoons chutney

2 teaspoons curry powder

1 teaspoon salt

1½ cups water

1 tablespoon cornflour (optional)

steamed rice or baked jacket potatoes, to serve

Peel the onions and carrot, and finely dice along with the celery and zucchini, if using. Place in the slow cooker.

Slice the sausages into 1 cm lengths and add to the cooker with the tomato, soy sauce, tomato sauce, jam, chutney, curry powder, salt and water.

Place lid on cooker and cook for 3½ hours on High or 7 hours on Low.

If necessary, mix the cornflour with about 2 tablespoons of cold water to a paste and use a little or all of it to thicken the dish. Add salt and pepper to taste.

Serve over steamed rice or baked jacket potatoes.

FRAGRANT PORK CURRY

Serves 6

2 onions
3 cloves garlic
1 kg lean diced pork
1 tablespoon ground cumin
1 tablespoon ground coriander
1 tablespoon ground turmeric
½ teaspoon ground cardamom
1 star anise
1 cup diced tomato
1 tablespoon Worcestershire sauce
3 teaspoons sweet chilli sauce
3 teaspoons plum sauce
3 teaspoons soy sauce
1 tablespoon chutney
3 teaspoons peanut butter (optional)
1 teaspoon salt
½ cup coconut cream
3 teaspoons cornflour

Peel and dice the onions. Peel and crush the garlic. Place in the slow cooker with the pork, cumin, coriander, turmeric, cardamom, star anise, tomato, Worcestershire sauce, sweet chilli sauce, plum sauce, soy sauce, chutney, peanut butter, if using, and salt. Stir to combine.

Place lid on cooker and cook for 5–6 hours on High or 10–11 hours on Low.

Stir in the coconut cream. If necessary, mix the cornflour with about 2 tablespoons of cold water to a paste and use a little or all of it to thicken the curry. Add salt and pepper to taste.

CREAMY PORK AND RED PEPPERS

Serves 4–6

500 g red capsicums
1 onion
3 cloves garlic
250 g tomatoes
800 g lean diced pork
1 teaspoon chicken or vegetable stock powder
1½ teaspoons salt
1 tablespoon chutney
½ cup stock
1 teaspoon sugar
1 tablespoon tomato paste
1 tablespoon paprika
1 tablespoon cornflour (optional)
⅔ cup sour cream
¼ cup finely chopped parsley
mashed potatoes and seasonal vegetables, to serve

Remove stalks, seeds and membranes from the capsicums and cut into 1 cm dice. Peel and dice the onion. Peel and crush the garlic. Dice the tomatoes. Place in the slow cooker and add the pork, stock powder, salt, chutney, stock, sugar, tomato paste and paprika.

Place lid on cooker and cook for 4 hours on High or 7–8 hours on Low. If necessary, mix the cornflour with about 2 tablespoons of cold water to a paste and use a little or all of it to thicken the mixture.

Stir in sour cream and add salt and pepper to taste. Sprinkle with parsley and serve with mashed potatoes and seasonal vegetables.

ROAST PORK WITH PRUNES AND APRICOT JUS

Serves 4–6

1.5 kg pork roast
1 small onion
8 prunes
1 cup fresh breadcrumbs
1 tablespoon chopped fresh sage
1 egg
½ teaspoon salt
pinch of dried sage (optional)
½ cup apricot nectar
1 teaspoon stock powder
2 teaspoons lemon juice
2 teaspoons tomato sauce (ketchup)
3 teaspoons sweet chilli sauce
2 teaspoons Dijon mustard
2 teaspoons cornflour (optional)

Remove all fat from the pork and cut a pocket part way through the centre.

Peel and grate the onion. Remove stones from prunes and chop. Combine with the breadcrumbs, sage, egg, salt and dried sage, if using. Stuff into the pocket in the pork and tie up the roast with string to enclose the filling.

Spray the slow cooker with cooking oil or grease lightly with butter. Place the roast in the cooker. Combine the apricot nectar, stock powder, lemon juice, tomato sauce, sweet chilli sauce and mustard. Pour over the pork.

Place lid on cooker and cook for 5 hours on High or 9–10 hours on Low.

Remove pork from cooker, retaining the juices, and leave to rest.

To make the jus, strain the juices from the cooker into a small saucepan. Bring to the boil and reduce until about 1 cup remains.

If necessary, mix the cornflour with about 1 tablespoon of cold water to a paste and use a little or all of it to thicken the jus. Add salt and pepper to taste.

ITALIAN MEATBALLS

Serves 4

2 eggs
½ onion
350 g lean pork mince
150 g beef sausage mince
½ cup fresh breadcrumbs
2 tablespoons flour
2 tablespoons ricotta
2 teaspoons plum sauce
1 tablespoon chopped parsley
1 tablespoon chopped basil
1 teaspoon salt

Sauce

½ onion
400 g canned or bottled diced tomato
2 tablespoons red wine
2 tablespoons tomato sauce (ketchup)
2 teaspoons Worcestershire sauce
2 teaspoons plum sauce
2 teaspoons paprika
2 teaspoons brown sugar
1 teaspoon salt

To make the meatballs, whisk the eggs and very finely dice or grate the onion. Add the remaining meatball ingredients. Mix well and roll into walnut-size balls.

To make the sauce, dice the onion and place in a separate bowl with the remaining ingredients.

Spoon 3 tablespoons of the sauce in the base of the slow cooker. Place a layer of meatballs on top, leaving a small space between them. Drizzle a little of the sauce over, add another layer of meatballs and cover evenly with the rest of the sauce.

Place lid on cooker and cook for 4 hours on High or 7–8 hours on Low.

MEAT ROLL WITH SPINACH AND BACON STUFFING

Serves 6

125 g chorizo sausage
1 small onion
1 clove garlic
1 egg
500 g beef mince
300 g lean pork mince
1 cup fresh breadcrumbs
2 teaspoons tomato sauce (ketchup)
2 teaspoons sweet chilli sauce
1 tablespoon plain flour
1 teaspoon salt
½ cup diced canned or bottled tomatoes
1 tablespoon tomato paste
1 teaspoon salt
1 teaspoon sugar

Spinach and Bacon Stuffing
¼ cup pitted kalamata olives
¼ cup semi-dried tomatoes
3 tablespoons pine nuts
120 g lean rindless bacon
60 g baby spinach leaves
1 egg, lightly whisked
1 tablespoon plain flour
5 tablespoons grated parmesan cheese

Remove skin from the chorizo and chop very finely. Peel and grate the onion. Peel and crush the garlic. Whisk the egg until well broken up. Place all in a bowl with the beef and pork mince, breadcrumbs, tomato sauce, chilli sauce, flour and salt and combine well. Set aside while preparing the stuffing.

To make the spinach and bacon stuffing, chop the olives, semi-dried tomatoes, pine nuts and bacon, and place in a bowl. Pour boiling water over the spinach leaves in a separate bowl and leave to stand for 1 minute. Drain. When cool enough to handle, squeeze out all moisture from spinach and chop finely. Add to the bacon mixture with the egg, flour and parmesan. If you wish, add ½ teaspoon of salt.

Spread a piece of plastic wrap approximately 50 cm long on a board or bench. Place the meat mixture onto it and pat out to a rectangle about 25 cm x 15 cm. Spread the stuffing evenly over the meat, leaving a 1 cm rim around the edges. Roll up from the narrow edge by lifting the edge of the plastic wrap to start the rolling and guide the rest of the way. Seal ends by pressing together firmly. Carefully lift the roll into the slow cooker, removing the plastic wrap.

Mix together the tomato, tomato paste, salt and sugar and spread over the top of the meat roll.

Place lid on cooker and cook for 4 hours on High or 7–8 hours on Low.

Slice the meat roll in the cooker, or remove with care and slice to serve.

PORK AND POLENTA PIE

Serves 6

1 onion
2 cloves garlic
1 red capsicum
1 tablespoon olive oil
500 g lean pork mince
1 tablespoon Worcestershire sauce
1 tablespoon sweet chilli sauce
2 teaspoons zucchini pickle
   (or other well-flavoured pickle)
1½ teaspoons paprika
1½ teaspoons salt
1 tablespoon polenta
1 cup fresh or frozen corn kernels
1¾ cups diced fresh, canned or bottled tomatoes
3 tablespoons tomato paste
2 teaspoons cornflour
½ cup grated tasty cheese

Polenta Topping
1 egg
1 cup milk
60 g ricotta
1½ cups self-raising flour
½ cup polenta
1 tablespoon grated parmesan cheese
¾ teaspoon salt
30 g melted butter

Peel and finely dice the onion. Peel and crush the garlic. Remove the stalk, seeds and membrane from the capsicum and dice.

Heat the oil in a heavy-based saucepan and lightly brown the mince. Add the onion, garlic and capsicum and cook for a further minute. Transfer mixture to the slow cooker. Add the Worcestershire sauce, sweet chilli sauce, zucchini pickle, 1 teaspoon paprika, salt, polenta, corn, tomato and tomato paste. Stir to combine.

Place lid on cooker and cook for 2 hours on High.

Mix the cornflour with about 1 tablespoon of cold water to a paste and use a little or all of it to thicken the mixture. Add salt and pepper to taste. Replace the lid.

To make the polenta topping, whisk the egg, milk and ricotta together until well combined. Mix in the flour, polenta, parmesan, salt and melted butter. Stir until very smooth, then spoon evenly over the meat mixture. Sprinkle with the tasty cheese and remaining paprika.

Replace lid and cook for 1½ hours on High, or until the topping is set.

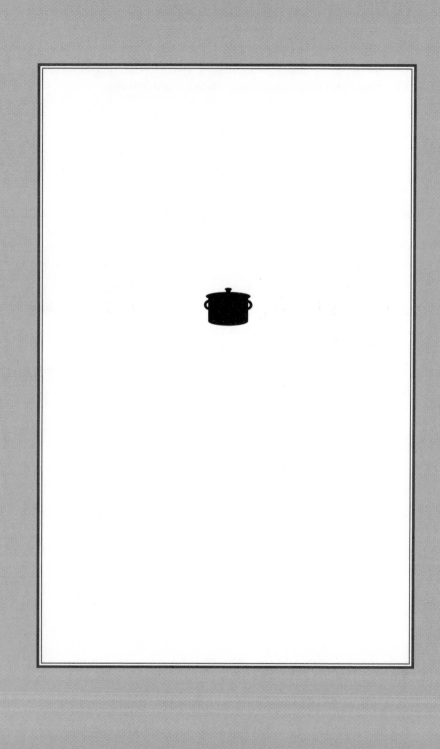

SEAFOOD

SPANISH-STYLE STUFFED SQUID WITH CREAMY POTATO CASSEROLE

Serves 4

The slow cooker is an ideal way to cook squid – the extended cooking time tenderises and moistens it, making it succulent and delicious. In this recipe, the stuffed squid is cooked on a bed of diced potato to form a delicious potato casserole as the squid is gently slow-cooked.

100 g chorizo sausage

90 g leek (white part only)

2 tomatoes

1 clove garlic

2 teaspoons olive oil

¼ cup diced bacon

1 egg

½ teaspoon finely diced preserved lemon rind,
    or 1 teaspoon finely grated lemon rind

¼ cup finely shredded basil leaves

1 cup fresh breadcrumbs

4 medium squid tubes, cleaned

750 g potatoes

¼ cup chicken or fish stock

30 g butter, cut into small pieces

juice of ½ lemon

3 teaspoons cornflour

1 tablespoon sour cream
1 teaspoon mayonnaise (optional)
1½ tablespoons chopped parsley

Dice the chorizo very finely. Wash the leek well and dice finely, along with the tomatoes. Peel and crush the garlic.

Heat the oil and sauté the chorizo, bacon and leek for 5 minutes, then add the tomato and garlic and sauté for a further 3 minutes. Lightly whisk the egg. Add to the sautéed mixture with the preserved lemon, basil and breadcrumbs. Mix well.

Use the mixture to stuff the squid tubes, leaving a little space at each end of the tube. Set aside while preparing the potatoes.

Turn the slow cooker setting to High. Peel the potatoes and cut into 1 cm dice. Place in base of cooker with the stock and butter. Stir to combine. Place the filled squid tubes on the potato mixture and drizzle over the lemon juice.

Place lid on cooker, turn setting to Low and cook for 3 hours.

Remove squid tubes to a dish. Mix the cornflour with about 2 tablespoons of cold water and use a little or all of it to thicken the potato mixture. Mix in the sour cream, mayonnaise, if using, and parsley.

Slice the squid and serve with the creamy potato casserole on the side.

AROMATIC FISH CURRY

Serves 4

600 g firm-fleshed fish fillets
1 small onion
2 tablespoons very finely diced leek
1 tablespoon very finely diced lemongrass
1 teaspoon ground cumin
1 teaspoon ground coriander
½ teaspoon garam masala
½ teaspoon ground cardamom
1 teaspoon ground turmeric
3 teaspoons sweet chilli sauce
2 teaspoons chutney
¾ cup coconut milk
½ teaspoon salt
2 teaspoons cornflour
1½ tablespoons chopped coriander

Cut the fish into 2.5 cm dice and place in the slow cooker. Peel and very finely dice the onion and add to the cooker with the leek, lemongrass, cumin, coriander, garam masala, cardamom, turmeric, sweet chilli sauce, chutney, ¼ cup of coconut milk and salt.

Place lid on cooker and cook for 2–2½ hours on Low.

Mix the remaining coconut milk with the cornflour until smooth. Place in a small saucepan and bring to the boil, stirring until it thickens. Stir into the curry in the cooker. Scatter the curry with the coriander and serve on steamed rice.

SALMON CUTLETS WITH DRIED FRUIT AND LIME

Serves 4

2 teaspoons very finely diced lemongrass
1 teaspoon olive oil
juice of 1 lime
1 teaspoon finely grated lime rind
4 salmon cutlets
1 small onion
¾ cup chopped dried apricots
¼ cup chopped raisins
2 teaspoons seeded mustard
1 teaspoon redcurrant or quince jelly
¼ cup white wine
¼ cup apricot nectar
2 teaspoons cornflour

Place 1 teaspoon of lemongrass, oil, lime juice and rind in base of slow cooker. Place the salmon cutlets on top.

Peel and very finely dice the onion. Place in a bowl with the remaining lemongrass, dried apricots, raisins, mustard and reducurrant or quince jelly. Spread evenly over the fish.

Mix together the white wine and apricot nectar and pour over the fish.

Place lid on cooker and cook for 2–2½ hours on Low.

Meanwhile, mix the cornflour with about 2 tablespoons of cold water to a paste.

Remove fish from cooker.

Immediately thicken the mixture in the cooker with a little or all of the cornflour paste. Add salt and pepper to taste, if required.

Place a small amount of the fruit mixture on each serving plate, top with a salmon cutlet and drizzle with a little of the jus from the cooker.

OCEAN TROUT FILLETS WITH SPICY ASIAN GLAZE

Serves 4

600 g ocean trout fillets
1 spring onion, white part only
1 clove garlic
1 teaspoon grated green ginger
2 tablespoons sherry
1 tablespoon soy sauce
2 teaspoons honey
1 teaspoon cornflour

Cut the fish into 10 cm x 5 cm pieces. Place in the slow cooker. Slice the spring onion and scatter over the fish.

Peel and crush the garlic. Place in a bowl with the ginger, sherry, soy sauce and honey and mix to combine. Pour over the fish.

Place lid on cooker and cook for 2–2½ hours on Low.

Remove fish to a serving dish.

Mix the cornflour with about 1 tablespoon of cold water to a paste. Pour the juices in the cooker into a small saucepan. Bring to the boil and thicken with the cornflour paste to make a glaze. Cook for a further minute. Add a little salt, if needed. Spoon a little of the glaze over each portion of fish.

WHOLE OCEAN TROUT WITH APRICOT AND ALMOND STUFFING

Serves 4–6

1 small onion
1 tablespoon finely chopped fennel
2 tablespoons chopped dried apricots
2 tablespoons finely chopped almonds
2 tablespoons lime juice
1 teaspoon finely grated lime rind
1 tablespoon chopped parsley
½ teaspoon salt
1 egg
1 ocean trout or similar firm-fleshed fish,
   cleaned and scaled

To make the stuffing, peel and very finely dice the onion. Place in a bowl with the fennel, apricot, almonds, lime juice and rind, parsley and salt. Lightly whisk the egg and combine with the other stuffing ingredients. Stuff the fish with this mixture.

In the slow cooker, place a piece of baking paper large enough to cover the base and most of the way up the sides. Place the fish on this.

Place lid on cooker and cook for 2½ hours on Low.

Note: *Choose a fish that will fit in your cooker — it may be necessary to remove the head and tail.*

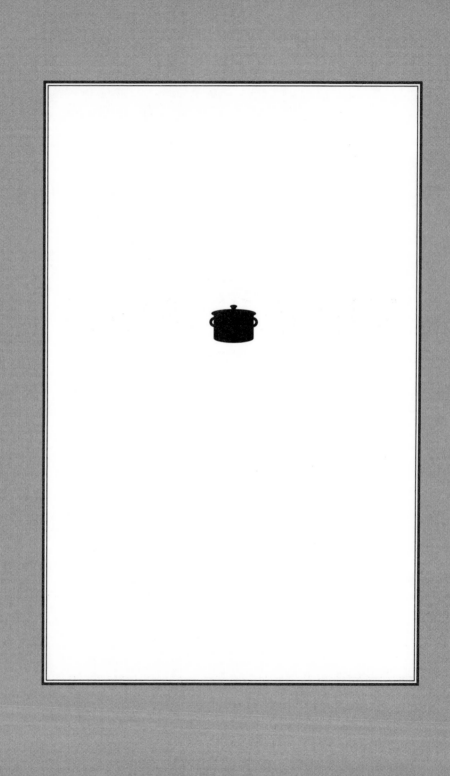

VEGETABLES

MINTED BABY POTATOES

Serves 4–6

1 kg small potatoes, such as Pink Eyes
2 tablespoons softened butter, plus 1 tablespoon extra
½ teaspoon salt
3 tablespoons finely chopped mint

Scrub the potatoes very well, or peel them if you prefer, and place in the slow cooker with the softened butter and salt.

Place lid on cooker and cook for 2–3 hours on High or 4 hours on Low.

Drain off any liquid from the cooker and add the extra butter and mint. Stir carefully to combine. Add salt and pepper to taste.

Paprika Potatoes

Serves 6

1.5 kg potatoes
1 onion
2 cloves garlic
3 teaspoons paprika
1½ teaspoons seeded mustard
1 tablespoon tomato sauce (ketchup)
1 cup stock
1 teaspoon lemon juice
1 teaspoon Worcestershire sauce
½ teaspoon salt
3 tablespoons sour cream
3 teaspoons cornflour (optional)

Peel the potatoes and cut into 1.5 cm dice. Peel and dice the onion, and peel and crush the garlic. Add to the slow cooker with the paprika, mustard, tomato sauce, stock, lemon juice, Worcestershire sauce and salt.

Place lid on cooker and cook for 3 hours on High or 6 hours on Low.

Turn off the heat and stir through the sour cream.

If necessary, mix the cornflour with about ¼ cup of cold water to a paste and use a little or all of it to thicken the dish. Add salt and pepper to taste.

MEDITERRANEAN POTATOES WITH OLIVES

Serves 4–6

2 onions
2 cloves garlic
750 g potatoes
1 large red capsicum
1 cup pitted kalamata olives
1¾ cups diced fresh, canned or bottled tomatoes
3 tablespoons tomato paste
3 teaspoons chutney
1½ teaspoons salt
1 teaspoon sugar
3 teaspoons cornflour (optional)

Peel and dice the onions. Peel and crush the garlic. Peel and cut the potatoes into 1 cm dice. Place in the slow cooker with the remaining ingredients and stir to combine.

Place lid on cooker and cook for 4–4½ hours on High or 8–9 hours on Low.

If necessary, mix the cornflour with about ¼ cup of cold water to a paste and use a little or all of it to thicken the dish. Add salt and pepper to taste.

Hot Potato Salad

Serves 6

1 kg potatoes
1 onion
2 cloves garlic
180 g lean bacon
1 teaspoon salt
½ cup chicken stock
1 tablespoon cornflour
½ cup cold milk
1 cup cream
2 teaspoons dijon or seeded mustard
2 teaspoons cider vinegar
1 cup grated tasty cheese
2 tablespoons finely chopped parsley

Peel the potatoes and cut into 1.25 cm dice. Peel and finely dice the onion. Peel and crush the garlic. Remove rind from bacon and dice. Place in the slow cooker and add the salt and chicken stock.

Place lid on cooker and cook for 3 hours on High or 6 hours on Low.

When cooking time is almost complete, mix the cornflour with the milk to a paste. Heat the cream until boiling and thicken with the cornflour paste. Mix in the mustard, vinegar and cheese. Stir until cheese is melted.

Remove lid from cooker and stir in the cheese sauce. Mix well.

Serve topped with chopped parsley.

SWEDE AND POTATO MASH

Serves 6

750 g swedes
500 g potatoes
1 small onion
60 g lean rindless bacon
1 teaspoon salt
¼ cup chicken stock or water
2 large tablepoons sour cream
chopped parsley, to serve

Peel the swedes, potatoes and onion, then cut into 1.25 cm dice. Dice the bacon. Place in the slow cooker with the salt and stock.

Place lid on cooker and cook for 5 hours on High or 8 hours on Low.

Purée the mixture until very smooth. Stir in the sour cream. Add salt and pepper to taste. Serve topped with a little chopped parsley.

Parsnip and Parmesan Mash

Serves 4–6

1 kg parsnips
¼ cup stock or water
60 g butter
¾ teaspoon salt
1½ teaspoons lemon juice
2 tablespoons cream
2 teaspoons grated parmesan cheese

Peel the parsnips and cut into thin strips. If the inner core of any parsnip is tough or stringy, discard it and use an extra parsnip to make up the lost weight.

Place in the slow cooker with the stock or water, half of the butter and the salt.

Place lid on cooker and cook for 3 hours on High or 5 hours on Low, or until parsnip is very soft.

Add the remaining butter and puree until smooth. Whisk in the lemon juice, cream and parmesan. Add salt and pepper to taste.

SWEET POTATO AND ROSEMARY PURÉE

Serves 4–6

1 kg peeled sweet potato
1 clove garlic
¾ cup chicken stock
juice of ½ orange
2 teaspoons lemon juice
2 teaspoons butter
1½ teaspoons salt
1½ tablespoons sour cream
1 tablespoon cream (optional)
2 teaspoons very finely chopped
    fresh rosemary leaves
toasted pine nuts, to serve (optional)

Cut the sweet potato into 3 cm pieces and place in the slow cooker.
Peel and crush the garlic and add to the potato, along with the
chicken stock, orange juice, lemon juice, butter and salt. Stir to
combine.

Place lid on cooker and cook for 4 hours on High or 8 hours on Low,
or until the sweet potato is very soft.

Purée the mixture. Stir through the sour cream, cream, if using, and
rosemary. Add salt and white pepper to taste. Serve scattered with
toasted pine nuts, if using.

BRUSSELS SPROUTS WITH HONEY AND BACON

Serves 4

400 g Brussels sprouts
3 tablespoons chicken stock
1 teaspoon seeded mustard
1 teaspoon honey
1 small onion
125 g rindless bacon
2 teaspoons oil

Cut the bases from the Brussels sprouts, remove any tough outer leaves and cut in half. Mix the stock with honey and mustard. Drizzle a small amount in base of slow cooker and add sprouts, cut-side up.

Peel and finely dice the onion. Dice the bacon. Heat the oil in a small saucepan and sauté the onion and bacon until the onion is transparent. Scatter over the sprouts. Drizzle with the rest of the stock, honey and mustard mixture.

Place lid on cooker and cook on High for 1½ hours, or until sprouts are tender.

HONEY CARROTS WITH CITRUS AND PARSLEY

Serves 4–6

750 g carrots
½ teaspoon grated orange rind
½ cup orange juice
2 teaspoons lemon juice
½ teaspoon salt
1 tablespoon honey
2 teaspoons butter
1–2 tablespoons finely chopped parsley

Peel the carrots and cut into thin strips. Place in the slow cooker with the orange rind, orange juice, lemon juice and salt. Drizzle over the honey.

Place lid on cooker and cook for 3 hours on High, or until carrot is just tender (check after 2½ hours).

Remove carrot from cooking liquid with a slotted spoon and place in a serving dish. Cut the butter into 4–6 pieces and stir through the carrot to coat. Add salt and pepper to taste, then stir through the parsley.

CABBAGE SAVOURY

Serves 4

4 cups shredded cabbage, firmly packed
2 onions
2 carrots
1½ stalks celery
180 g bacon, rind removed
1 tablespoon cider vinegar
1 teaspoon sugar
½ teaspoon salt

Place cabbage in the slow cooker.

Peel the onions and carrots and finely dice. Dice the celery and bacon. Add to the cooker with the vinegar, sugar and salt. Mix well.

Place lid on cooker and cook for 2–3 hours on High.

Stir and add salt and pepper to taste.

RED CABBAGE AND BACON BRAISE

Serves 4

1 onion
1 apple
150 g diced bacon
5 cups finely shredded red cabbage
1 teaspoon sugar
½ teaspoon salt
1 teaspoon caraway seeds
1 tablespoon cider vinegar
30 g butter

Peel and finely dice the onion. Peel, core and dice the apple. Place all in the slow cooker with the bacon and cabbage. Add the sugar, salt, caraway seeds, vinegar and 1 tablespoon of water. Mix well.

Cut the butter into small pieces and dot over the top of the cabbage mixture.

Place lid on cooker and cook for 2 hours on High.

Add salt and pepper to taste.

Medley of Vegetables in Cheese and Parsley Sauce

Serves 4–6

1 kg mixed fresh vegetables, such as parsnips, carrots,
    sweet potato, celery
1 cup stock, or water with 2 teaspoons stock powder
1½ tablespoons cornflour
1⅓ cups milk
1 cup grated tasty cheese
2 teaspoons dijon mustard
3 tablespoons chopped parsley

Peel all the vegetables and cut into 1 cm dice. Place in the slow
cooker with the stock.

Place lid on cooker and cook for 3 hours on High or 6 hours on Low.

Near the end of cooking time, mix the cornflour with ½ cup of the
milk to a paste. Heat the remaining milk until boiling and quickly
whisk in the cornflour paste. Stir in the cheese and mustard.

When the vegetables are cooked, stir the cheese sauce through,
together with the chopped parsley.

POLENTA

Serves 6

1½ cups polenta
2½ cups milk
2½ cups water
1½ teaspoons salt
½ cup cream
1 cup grated parmesan cheese

Place the polenta in the slow cooker.

Place the milk, water and salt in a saucepan and bring to the boil.
Pour over the polenta.

Place lid on cooker and cook for 1¼ hours on High or 2½ hours on
Low.

Stir in the cream and parmesan. Add salt to taste.

Note: *You may need to add a little extra cream, milk or water to bring the dish
to the consistency you require.*

Pilaf

Serves 4–5

2 onions
4 cloves garlic
2 cups long grain rice
5 cups warm chicken stock, or water with
    1 tablespoon stock powder
2 teaspoons dried basil

Peel and finely dice the onions. Peel and crush the garlic.

Place all ingredients in the slow cooker and stir to combine.

Place lid on cooker and cook for 2 hours on High or 3½–4 hours on Low.

Add salt and pepper to taste.

PUMPKIN RISOTTO

Serves 4–6

1 large onion
1 clove garlic
1 cup arborio rice
2½ cups chicken stock, or water with
   3 teaspoons stock powder
1 cup pureed cooked pumpkin
¾ cup grated parmesan cheese
½ cup milk
½ cup cream
2 teaspoons lemon juice

Peel and finely dice the onion. Peel and crush the garlic. Place in the slow cooker with the rice and stock and mix well.

Place lid on cooker and cook for 2½–3 hours on High or 4–5 hours on Low.

Stir and fold in the pumpkin, parmesan, milk, cream and lemon juice until well combined. Add salt and pepper to taste.

Homemade Baked Beans

Serves 6

This is a recipe developed by our 16-year-old-daughter, Courtney, which she has adapted here for the slow cooker. It's extremely easy to prepare, nutritious and so delicious that you will never again return to the canned variety.

> 500 g dried haricot or navy beans
> 2 onions
> 3½ cups tomato purée
> 3 tablespoons tomato paste
> 1½ tablespoons mild-flavoured honey
> 3 teaspoons vegetable stock powder

Cover the beans with cold water (at least 3 cm). Leave to soak overnight. The next day, drain off the liquid. Cook for 15 minutes in boiling water. Drain.

Peel and finely dice the onion and place in the slow cooker with the beans, 1 cup of water, tomato purée, tomato paste, honey and stock powder.

Place lid on cooker and cook for 4 hours on High or 7 hours on Low.

Note: *For variation, add a smoked ham hock to the cooker along with the rest of the ingredients for a lovely rich, meaty sauce. Extend the cooking time on Low to 8 hours if you do this. When ready to serve, remove the hock from the cooker, take the meat from the bone and return it to the baked bean mixture.*

DHAL

Serves 4–6

1 onion
1 clove garlic
2 tomatoes
180 g red lentils
2 teaspoons ground cumin
2 teaspoons ground coriander
1 teaspoon ground turmeric
3 cups stock or water
1 teaspoon salt
3 teaspoons sweet chilli sauce
3 teaspoons tomato chutney
½ cup coconut cream

Peel and dice the onion. Peel and crush the garlic. Dice the tomatoes. Place in the slow cooker with the lentils, cumin, coriander, turmeric, stock or water and salt. Stir to combine.

Place lid on cooker and cook for 6 hours on Low.

Stir through the sweet chilli sauce, chutney and coconut cream. Add salt and pepper to taste.

Spiced Lentils

Serves 4–6

This dish has been a specialty of our daughter Courtney since she first invented it when she was 12 years old. It remains a household favourite and is ideal as a vegetarian main course. She has adapted the recipe here for the slow cooker.

> 1 cup green lentils
> 3 cups water
> 2 teaspoons coriander seeds
> 2 teaspoons cumin seeds
> ½ teaspoon whole cloves
> 1 teaspoon ground turmeric
> ½ teaspoon cayenne pepper
> 1 teaspoon sugar
> 1½ teaspoons salt
> 1 cup crushed fresh, canned
>   or bottled tomatoes
> 1 large tablespoon tomato paste
> 1 onion
> 1 carrot
> 4 cloves garlic

Combine the lentils and water in a bowl and leave to soak overnight.

The next day, pour the lentils and water mixture into the slow cooker.

In a mortar and pestle or spice grinder, grind to a powder the coriander and cumin seeds and cloves. Add to the cooker with the turmeric, cayenne pepper, sugar, salt, tomato and tomato paste.

Peel the onion and carrot and dice finely. Peel and crush the garlic. Add to the cooker and stir to combine.

Place lid on cooker and cook for 8–9 hours on Low. Add salt and pepper to taste.

SPICY PUMPKIN CURRY

Serves 4–6

When cooked, this curry will contain a pumpkin puree, as well as defined pieces of pumpkin.

750 g pumpkin
1 onion
2 cloves garlic
1 cup chicken or vegetable stock,
    or water with 2 teaspoons stock powder
1 teaspoon ground coriander
2 teaspoons ground cumin
½ fenugreek teaspoon ground
½ teaspoon ground fennel
½ teaspoon ground turmeric
½ teaspoon dried mint
2 teaspoons chutney
1 tablespoon tomato paste
1 teaspoon salt
½ cup coconut cream
2 teaspoons cornflour (optional)

Peel the pumpkin and cut into 2 cm pieces. Peel and chop the onion. Peel and crush the garlic. Place in the slow cooker with the stock, coriander, cumin, fenugreek, fennel, turmeric, mint, chutney, tomato paste and salt. Mix well.

Place lid on cooker and cook for 3 hours on High or 5½ hours on Low.

Stir in the coconut cream. Add salt and pepper to taste.

If necessary, mix the cornflour with about 1½ tablespoons of cold water to a paste and use a little or all of it to thicken the curry.

Vegetarian Curry with Tofu

Serves 4–6

1 onion
1 kg vegetables, such as pumpkin, sweet potato, carrot,
   parsnip, potato, kohlrabi, cauliflower
1 clove garlic
1 long red chilli (optional)
2 teaspoons ground cumin
1 teaspoon ground coriander
1 teaspoon turmeric
½ teaspoon ground cardamom
½ teaspoon garam masala
1 star anise
2 teaspoons stock powder
1 teaspoon finely grated green ginger root
¾ cup fresh, canned or bottled diced tomato
2 tablespoons tomato paste
2 tablespoons sweet chilli sauce
350 g tofu, cut into 1.5 cm cubes
1 tablespoon cornflour
½ cup coconut cream

Peel the onion and vegetables (as appropriate) and cut into 1.5 cm
dice. Break cauliflower, if using, into florets. Peel and crush the garlic.
Remove stalk end, seeds and membrane from the chilli, if using, and
chop finely. Place all in the slow cooker.

Add the cumin, coriander, turmeric, cardamom, garam masala, star anise, stock powder or salt, ginger, tomato, tomato paste, sweet chilli sauce and ½ cup water. Mix well.

Add the tofu and stir through carefully.

Place lid on cooker and cook for 4 hours on High or 7–8 hours on Low.

Mix the cornflour with about 3 tablespoons of cold water to a paste and use a little or all of it to thicken the mixture. Stir in the coconut cream. Add salt and pepper to taste.

Spicy Cauliflower, Potato and Pea Curry

Serves 6

1 onion
3 cloves garlic
750 g potatoes
375 g cauliflower florets
juice of 1 lime or lemon
½ teaspoon finely grated lime or lemon rind
3 teaspoons zucchini pickle
   (or other well-flavoured pickle)
2 teaspoons ground cumin
1 teaspoon ground coriander
1 teaspoon curry powder
1 cup coconut milk
½ cup coconut cream
1½ cups fresh or frozen peas
2 long red chillies (optional)
3 teaspoons tomato chutney
3 teaspoons seeded mustard
1 tablespoon tomato sauce (ketchup)
2 teaspoons golden syrup
1 tablespoon cornflour (optional)
2 tablespoons natural yoghurt
finely chopped mint, to serve

Peel and finely dice the onion. Peel and crush the garlic. Peel the potatoes and cut into 1 cm dice. Place all in the slow cooker with the cauliflower, lime or lemon juice and rind, zucchini pickle, cumin, coriander, curry powder and coconut milk.

Place lid on cooker and cook for 4 hours on High.

Stir in the coconut cream, then add the peas. Finely dice the chillies, if using, and stir through. Replace lid and cook for a further 30 minutes.

Stir in the chutney, mustard, tomato sauce and golden syrup. If necessary, mix the cornflour with about 2 tablespoons of cold water to a paste and use a little or all of it to thicken the curry. Stir in the yoghurt. Add salt and pepper to taste.

Serve sprinkled with a little chopped mint.

PEPERONATA

Serves 4–6

This is not a true peperonata, but it has come to be our home version, evolving over the years to make this tasty dish. It can be used as a vegetarian meal in its own right, or serves well as a side dish, or even as the tomato topping for a pizza.

    750 g red capsicums
    300 g tomatoes
    300 g zucchini
    2 onions
    4 cloves garlic
    ⅓ cup tomato paste
    1 tablespoons sweet chilli sauce
    1 tablespoon chutney
    1 teaspoon sugar
    1 teaspoon salt
    3–4 teaspoons cornflour (optional)

Remove the stalk, seeds and membrane from the capsicums and cut into 1.25 cm dice. Chop the tomatoes into 1.25 cm dice. Trim the zucchini and cut into 1.25 cm dice. Peel and finely dice the onions. Peel and crush the garlic.

Place vegetables in the slow cooker and add the tomato paste, sweet chilli sauce, chutney, sugar and salt. Stir to combine.

Place lid on cooker and cook for 4 hours on High or 7–8 hours on Low.

Add salt and pepper to taste. If necessary, mix the cornflour with about 2 tablespoons of cold water to a paste and use a little or all of it to thicken the dish.

Cannelloni with Spinach and Feta

Serves 4–6

250 g frozen spinach or fresh baby silverbeet leaves
1 small onion
375 g feta cheese, crumbled
1½ cups grated tasty cheese
¾ cup grated parmesan cheese
2 teaspoons chopped parsley
3 eggs
250 g instant cannelloni shells
3 cups diced canned or bottled tomatoes or passata
2 tablespoons tomato paste
1 teaspoon sugar
½ teaspoon salt

Cook the spinach or silverbeet in 3 tablespoons water for 3 minutes. Drain well and leave to cool, then squeeze to remove all liquid. Chop finely.

Peel and grate the onion. Combine the spinach and onion with the feta, 1 cup of tasty cheese, ½ cup of parmesan and the parsley. Whisk the eggs and mix through. Fill the cannelloni shells with this mixture.*

Mix together the tomato, tomato paste, sugar and salt. Spread a thin layer in the base of the slow cooker, and then put a layer of the cannelloni shells. Spread half the remaining tomato mixture, then the rest of the shells and top with the last of the tomato mixture. Combine the remaining tasty cheese and parmesan and scatter over the top.

Place lid on cooker and cook for 1½–2 hours on High.

Hint: *It is much easier to fill the cannelloni shells using a piping bag. Disposable piping bags are available at most supermarkets.*

Note: *Use a mixture of half feta, half ricotta if a little less saltiness is preferred. Personally, I like the sharp saltiness of the feta.*

Vegetarian Lasagne with Eggplant and Capsicum

Serves 4–6

400 g eggplant
1 tablespoon salt, plus 1½ teaspoons extra
500 g red capsicums
3 teaspoons cornflour
150 g mushrooms
1 onion
3 cloves garlic
810 g diced canned or bottled tomatoes
3 large tablespoons tomato paste
1 tablespoon chutney
3 teaspoons Worcestershire sauce
2 teaspoons soy sauce
3 teaspoons chilli sauce
1½ teaspoons sugar
250 g packet instant lasagne sheets
½ cup shredded basil leaves

Cheese Sauce
350 g ricotta
3 teaspoons cornflour
3 eggs
1 teaspoon salt
½ cup grated tasty cheese
1 cup grated fresh parmesan

Cut the eggplant into 6 mm slices. Place in a colander, sprinkle with the salt and mix well. Leave to stand for 30 minutes, then rinse and pat dry.

Mix the cornflour with about 2 tablespoons of cold water to a paste and set aside.

To prepare the tomato sauce, remove the stalks, seeds and membrane from the capsicums and cut into 2 cm dice. Place in a heatproof dish, cover with plastic wrap and microwave for 5 minutes on high. Drain off the liquid.

Wipe and dice the mushrooms. Peel and dice the onion. Peel and crush the garlic. Place in a medium saucepan with the tomato, tomato paste, chutney, Worcestershire sauce, soy sauce, chilli sauce, sugar and extra salt. Cook over medium-high heat, stirring often until sauce is reduced to two-thirds its original volume. Thicken with the cornflour paste.

To make the cheese sauce, whisk together the ricotta, cornflour, eggs and salt, then add the tasty cheese and half the parmesan.

Turn the slow cooker setting to High and spray with cooking oil or grease with butter. Spread 3 tablespoons of the tomato sauce over the base.

Top with one-third of the eggplant, then one-third of the lasagne sheets, broken into pieces to fit cooker, and spread with a little more tomato sauce. Then cover with half the remaining eggplant, then half the capsicum, half the basil, a small amount of tomato sauce and a small amount of the cheese sauce. Top with half the remaining lasagne sheets, spread with tomato sauce, and then layer with the remaining eggplant, capsicum and basil. Top with the rest of the tomato sauce, a layer of cheese sauce, then the last of the lasagne sheets, cheese sauce and parmesan.

Place lid on cooker and cook for 2 hours on High.

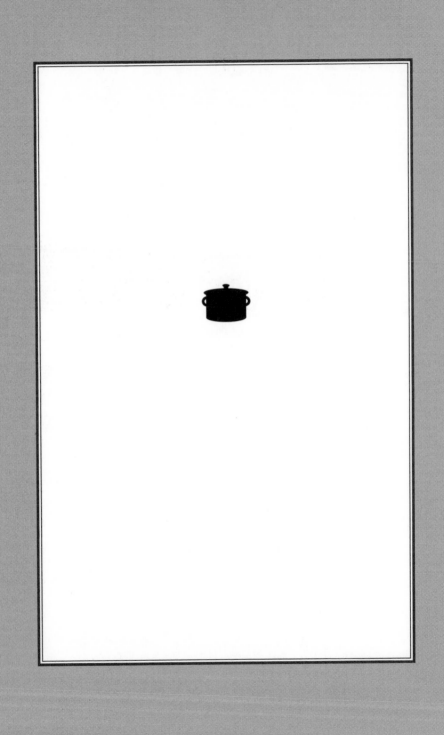

DESSERTS

CLASSIC BAKED APPLES

Serves 4–8

8 apples, such as Sturmer or Golden Delicious
3 teaspoons butter
¼ cup dates
½ cup sultanas
1½ tablespoons brown sugar
½ teaspoon ground cinnamon
1 tablespoon golden syrup

Core the apples and run a sharp knife around the middle of the apple, just to break the skin. Grease the slow cooker with 1 teaspoon of the butter and place apples inside.

Chop the dates and combine with the sultanas, brown sugar and cinnamon. Spoon into the cavity of the apples (don't worry if a little spills over the sides), pressing down gently.

Drizzle over the golden syrup, then top each apple with the remaining butter. Pour ½ cup of water around the apples (not over the top).

Place lid on cooker and cook for 3–4 hours on Low, or until the apples are cooked.

Mulled Pears

Serves 4–6

1¼ cups red wine
¼ cup lemon juice
1 cup sugar
½ cinnamon stick
4 cloves
small strip of lemon rind
6–8 pears
1 tablespoon cornflour*

Place the red wine, lemon juice, sugar, cinnamon stick, cloves and lemon rind in the slow cooker. Turn cooker setting to High and stir occasionally until sugar is dissolved.

Meanwhile, peel the pears, leaving the stalks intact. When syrup is ready, place pears in cooker. Place lid on cooker and cook for 1½ hours on High or 3 hours on Low.

Remove pears from cooker and place in a serving dish.

Place a sieve over a medium saucepan and strain the liquid from the cooker into it. Pour 1½ cups of the liquid into a small saucepan and bring to the boil. Mix the cornflour with about 2 tablespoons of cold water to a paste and use a little or all of it to slightly thicken the sauce. Spoon sauce over the pears.

Hint: *If you have access to arrowroot, use this in place of the cornflour as it will make for a clearer sauce. However, remove the sauce from the heat as soon as it has thickened.*

Lemon Sago

Serves 4–6

90 g sago or seed tapioca
2 teaspoons grated lemon rind
½ cup sugar
2 tablespoons golden syrup
juice of 1 large lemon

Place the sago, 2½ cups of water and lemon rind in the slow cooker and stir to combine.

Place lid on cooker and cook on High for about 45 minutes to 1 hour, or until sago is clear.

Turn off cooker and mix in the sugar, golden syrup and lemon juice.

SAGO PLUM PUDDING

Serves 6–8

⅓ cup sago or seed tapioca
1 cup milk
1 cup raisins
1 cup fresh breadcrumbs
½ cup brown sugar, firmly packed
1 teaspoon bicarbonate of soda
½ teaspoon vanilla essence
¼ cup melted butter
ice-cream, cream or custard, to serve

Mix the sago with milk and let stand for several hours or overnight.

When ready to make the pudding, grease a 4-cup capacity metal pudding basin. Combine the sago and milk with the raisins, breadcrumbs, brown sugar, bicarbonate of soda, vanilla and melted butter. Mix well and spoon into basin. Cover with two layers of foil and tie with string around rim of basin to secure foil and ensure a good seal.

Place pudding basin in slow cooker and pour boiling water into the cooker to two-thirds up the sides of the basin.

Place lid on cooker and cook for 4 hours on High.

Remove basin from cooker and leave to stand for 5 minutes before inverting pudding onto a serving plate.

This pudding is delicious served with ice-cream, cream or custard.

Lemon and Apple Brown Betty

Serves 4–6
(for a 3.5 litre slow cooker only)

1.5 kg cooking apples, such as Granny Smith,
    Sturmer or Bramley
1 tablespoon lemon juice
2 tablespoons sugar (optional)
10 slices bread, crusts removed
¾ cup brown sugar, firmly packed
1 teaspoon ground cinnamon
½ teaspoon ground nutmeg
grated rind of 1 lemon
125 g butter, melted

Grease the inside of the slow cooker with a little butter or spray with cooking oil.

Peel and core the apples. Cut each apple into quarters, then each quarter in half again. Place apple in the base of the cooker and drizzle with lemon juice. If the apples are quite sour, mix through the sugar.

Layer half the bread on a board and cut into four, lengthways, then into four, crossways. Repeat with remaining bread.

Place bread cubes in a large bowl and combine with the remaining ingredients, using two metal spoons to mix together well. Place over the top of the apple and spread out evenly.

Place lid on cooker and cook for 3–4 hours on Low.

Fruity Bread and Butter Custard

Serves 4–6
(for a 3.5 litre slow cooker only)

4 slices fruit bread
4 slices white or wholemeal bread
45 g butter, softened, plus 2 teaspoons extra
½ cup sultanas
½ cup chopped dried apricots
½ teaspoon finely grated lemon rind
4 large or 5 smaller eggs
¾ cup sugar
2 cups milk
½ teaspoon vanilla essence
¼ teaspoon ground nutmeg
1 tablespoon brown sugar
½ teaspoon ground cinnamon

Cut the crusts from the bread and spread each slice thinly with the butter. Cut into 2 cm squares and place in the slow cooker. Scatter over this the sultanas, apricots and lemon rind. Mix together gently.

Beat the eggs and sugar until well combined, then whisk in the milk and vanilla. Pour evenly over the bread mixture. Sprinkle with nutmeg.

Cut the extra butter into 8 pieces and dot over the top. Place lid on cooker and cook for 4 hours on Low or until the custard is set.

Combine the brown sugar and cinnamon and sprinkle evenly over the top of the pudding. Replace the lid and cook for a further 5 minutes, or until the sugar melts.

CLAFOUTIS

Serves 4–6
(for a 3.5 litre slower cooker only)

125 g fresh or frozen blueberries
125 g fresh or frozen raspberries
2 eggs
½ cup sugar
½ cup milk
½ cup self-raising flour
½ teaspoon grated lemon rind
90 g butter, melted
icing sugar, to dust
crème fraîche, cream or ice-cream, to serve

Grease the inside of the slow cooker with a little butter or spray with cooking oil.

Spread the berries evenly over the base. Whisk the eggs and sugar together until light and fluffy, then mix in all together the milk, flour, lemon rind and butter. Pour evenly over the berries.

Place lid on cooker and cook for 2 hours on High.

Dust with a little icing sugar and serve with crème fraîche, cream or ice-cream.

AUTUMN FRUITS COBBLER

Serves 6
(for a 4.5 litre slower cooker only)

8 cooking apples
2 large stalks rhubarb
1 tablespoon cornflour
1 tablespoon lemon juice
3 cups fresh, frozen or bottled blackberries
¼ cup sugar, plus extra to taste
1 egg
1 teaspoon finely grated lemon rind
1 tablespoon lemon juice
½ cup milk
1½ cups self-raising flour
125 g butter, melted
crème fraîche, ice-cream or yoghurt, to serve

Peel and core the apples and cut into chunks. Trim the rhubarb and
strip off any tough outer skin.

Mix the cornflour with about ¼ cup of cold water to a paste. Set aside.

Place the apple and rhubarb in a saucepan with the lemon juice
and ¼ cup of water. Bring to the boil, then simmer until the apple
is tender but not mushy. Add the blackberries, stir and cook for
1 minute, then add the extra sugar to taste. Bring back to the boil
and thicken with the cornflour paste. Pour mixture into the slow
cooker and turn setting down to Low.

Whisk the egg and sugar until creamy, then add the lemon rind, lemon juice, milk, flour and butter (all at once), and whisk until smooth. Place tablespoons of the mixture evenly over the fruit.

Place lid on cooker and cook for 2–3 hours on Low.

Serve with crème fraîche, ice-cream or yoghurt.

Note: *Any fruit can be used in place of those suggested in this recipe. In summer, try using gooseberries or mulberries for instance, in which case you may need to increase the amount of cornflour paste used to thicken the mixture, otherwise it will soak into the cobbler topping a little too much and make it soggy.*

BANANA SELF-SAUCING PUDDING

Serves 4–6
(for a 3.5 litre slow cooker only)

This pudding makes its own rich caramel sauce, in this case lightened by the pleasant addition of a hint of lime and a dash of lemon.

125 g butter
¾ cup sugar
1 egg
½ teaspoon ground cinnamon
½ teaspoon bicarbonate of soda
1½ cups self-raising flour
2 tablespoons lime juice
2 teaspoons grated lime rind
1 cup mashed ripe banana
1 teaspoon vanilla essence

Sauce
¾ cup brown sugar, firmly packed
1 teaspoon butter
3 tablespoons golden syrup
2 teaspoons lemon juice

Whisk the butter and sugar together until fluffy, then whisk in the egg. Mix in all the dry ingredients, lime juice and rind, mashed banana and vanilla essence to a smooth batter.

Pour mixture into the slow cooker and smooth out.

Place the brown sugar, butter, golden syrup, lemon juice and 1 cup of water in a saucepan. Bring to the boil, stirring, and pour evenly over the pudding batter.

Place lid on cooker and cook for 2–2¼ hours on High.

APPLE SELF-SAUCING PUDDING

Serves 4–6
(for a 3.5 litre slow cooker only)

4 cooking apples, such as Granny Smith
1 tablespoon butter
2 rounded tablespoons self-raising flour
¾ cup sugar
2 teaspoons lemon juice

Peel and core the apples, then cut in half lengthways.

Grease the inside of the slow cooker with a little butter or spray with cooking oil.

Place the apple cut-side up in the cooker.

Rub the butter into the flour with your fingertips. Mix in the sugar, ¾ cups of cold water and lemon juice (the mixture will look very unusual). Pour mixture evenly over the apple.

Place lid on cooker and cook for 2 hours on High or 4 hours on Low.

APRICOT GINGERBREAD PUDDING

Serves 4–6
(for a 4.5 litre slow cooker only)

1 large can apricot halves, or 1 bottle preserved apricots
1¾ cups self-raising flour
½ teaspoon bicarbonate of soda
½ teaspoon ground cinnamon
2 teaspoons ground ginger
1 egg
½ cup milk
3 teaspoons lemon juice
90 g butter
60 g brown sugar
½ cup golden syrup
ice-cream, crème fraîche or mascarpone, to serve

Drain the apricots, reserving ½ cup of the juice. Place the apricots and reserved juice in the base of slow cooker.

Place the flour, bicarbonate of soda, cinnamon and ginger in a bowl. Whisk in the egg with the milk and lemon juice. Melt the butter, brown sugar and golden syrup together in a small saucepan. Cool slightly and then mix into the bowl with the other ingredients. Pour mixture over the apricots.

Place lid on cooker and cook for 2 hours on High.

Serve with ice-cream, crème fraîche or mascarpone mixed with a little cream.

APPLE AND CINNAMON SPONGE PUDDING

Serves 4–6

1 kg apples
juice of 1 lemon
½ cup sugar, plus 2 teaspoons extra
2 teaspoons butter
½–1 teaspoon ground cinnamon
ice-cream, cream or yoghurt, to serve

Sponge Topping
1 egg
¾ cup sugar
½ cup milk
1½ cups self-raising flour
1 teaspoon grated lemon rind
2 tablespoons lemon juice
60 g butter, melted

Peel and core the apples and cut into eighths. Place in the slow cooker with the lemon juice, ½ cup of sugar and ¼ cup of water.

Place lid on cooker and cook for 2–3 hours on High or 4–5 hours on Low.*

Turn cooker setting to High while preparing the sponge topping. Whisk the egg and sugar together, then whisk in the milk, flour, lemon rind, lemon juice and melted butter (all at once). Pour evenly over the apple in the cooker.

Replace lid and cook for about 45 minutes to 1 hour on High, or until well risen and cooked through.

Remove lid from cooker and rub the butter over the surface of the sponge, then sprinkle with the extra sugar and cinnamon. Serve with ice-cream, cream or yoghurt.

Hint: *Alternatively, you can cook the apples on the stovetop, but will need to add about $^1/_4$ cup extra water. When cooked, place in the slow cooker while still hot and proceed with the recipe.*

Steamed Fruit Pudding

Serves 6

This recipe can quite easily serve as a Christmas pudding that can even be made just the day before it is needed. To lengthen its shelf life, brush the entire pudding with brandy while hot. When cool, wrap in foil. Place in the fridge where it will then keep well for a week or more.

1 cup dried mixed fruit
½ cup brown sugar, firmly packed
1 teaspoon mixed spice
¾ cup milk
1 tablespoon butter
1 tablespoon marmalade
2 tablespoons grated apple
1 teaspoon bicarbonate of soda
¼ cup brandy
1 cup self-raising flour

Brandy Custard
2 cups milk
½ cup sugar
2 tablespoons cornflour
2 egg yolks, whisked
1–2 tablespoons brandy

Grease a 4-cup capacity metal pudding basin. Line the base of the pudding basin with a circular piece of baking paper to fit in place. Then grease the baking paper with butter or spray with cooking oil.

Place the dried fruit, sugar, mixed spice, milk, butter, marmalade and apple in a medium saucepan. Bring to the boil, stirring, then simmer for 1 minute. Remove from heat, stir in the bicarbonate of soda and leave to cool for 10 minutes.

Fold in the brandy and flour until well combined. Pour mixture into the pudding basin. Cover basin with two layers of foil and tie with string around the rim of basin to secure foil and ensure a good seal.

Place pudding basin in cooker and pour boiling water into cooker to two-thirds of the way up the basin.

Place lid on cooker and cook for 3½ hours on High.

Remove basin from cooker, leave to stand for 5 minutes, then invert pudding onto a serving plate, or transfer onto a rack if it's to be used at a later date.

To make the brandy sauce, place the milk, sugar and cornflour in a saucepan and bring to the boil, stirring constantly. Cook until thickened. Remove from heat and quickly whisk in the egg yolks and brandy. Serve slices of pudding with brandy custard.

Rum and Raisin Pudding

Serves 4–6

¾ cup raisins
1½ tablespoons rum
125 g butter
1 cup sugar
2 eggs
3 tablespoons cocoa
½ cup self-raising flour
cream or ice-cream, to serve (optional)

Chocolate Ganache
250 g dark chocolate
250 ml cream
2 teaspoons butter (optional)

Soak the raisins in the rum for 30 minutes, if possible.

Grease a 4-cup capacity metal pudding basin. Line the base of the pudding basin with a circular piece of baking paper to fit in place. Then grease the baking paper with butter or spray with cooking oil.

Whisk the butter and sugar together until light and fluffy, then whisk in the eggs. Fold in the cocoa and flour, then fold in the rum and raisin mixture.

Spoon mixture into the pudding basin. Cover with two layers of foil and tie string around the basin just under the rim to secure the foil and ensure a good seal.

Place pudding basin in cooker and pour boiling water into the cooker to two-thirds up the sides of the basin.

Place lid on cooker and cook for 3 hours on High.

Remove basin from cooker, leave to stand for 10 minutes, then invert pudding onto a serving plate.

To make the chocolate ganache, break the chocolate into small pieces. Bring the cream to the boil, remove from heat and stir in the chocolate until melted and smooth. For an extra rich sauce and to give a lovely glossy finish, add the butter and stir until well combined.

Serve the pudding with the chocolate ganache for an extra rich dessert, or cream or ice-cream.

Mud Pudding with Whisky Sauce

Serves 6–8

150 g dark cooking chocolate
250 g butter
2 cups brown sugar, firmly packed
1 cup water
2 eggs
¼ cup cocoa
2 cups plain flour
2 teaspoons baking powder
ice-cream or cream, to serve

Whisky Sauce
200 g dark chocolate
200 ml cream
¼ cup whisky

Grease the inside of the slow cooker with a little butter or spray with cooking oil.

Break the chocolate into small squares and cut the butter into several pieces. Place in a medium saucepan with the sugar and water. Stir over medium heat until the butter and chocolate are melted and the sugar dissolved. Remove from heat and allow to cool for 5 minutes.

Whisk in the eggs, then the cocoa, flour and baking powder. Pour the mixture into the cooker.

Place lid on cooker and cook for 3 hours on High.

To make the whisky sauce, break the chocolate into small pieces. Place the cream in a medium saucepan and bring to the boil. Remove from heat and add the chocolate, stirring until melted. Add the whisky and stir to combine.

Serve slices of the pudding with a generous amount of whisky sauce and ice-cream or cream.

Note: *Any leftover sauce from this decadent but delicious dessert can be stored in a jar in the fridge. To melt, simply remove lid and microwave on medium for 20-second bursts. Serve over ice-cream.*

Black Forest Self-Saucing Pudding

Serves 6

This pudding has a sponge topping with a delicious chocolate cherry brandy sauce.

1½ cups canned or bottled pitted cherries,*
   with ½ cup juice reserved
1 tablespoon kirsch or brandy
1 cup self-raising flour
½ cup sugar
2½ tablespoons cocoa,
   plus 2 tablespoons extra
⅔ cup milk
1 teaspoon vanilla essence
1 egg
100g butter, melted
1 cup brown sugar, firmly packed
1¾ cups boiling water

Greast the inside of the slow cooker with a little butter or spray with cooking oil.

Combine the cherries, reserved juice and kirsch or brandy and place in base of cooker.

Place the flour, sugar and cocoa in a bowl and mix well. Whisk together the milk, vanilla and egg. Add to the flour mixture along with the melted butter and mix until well combined. Spoon this batter over the cherries and smooth out evenly.

To make the sauce, mix together the brown sugar and extra cocoa. Sprinkle evenly over the cake batter. Gently pour the boiling water over the top.

Place lid on cooker and cook for 2½ hours on High.

Hint: *Sour cherries are best for this recipe, but if you are unable to get them then sweet black cherries make a good substitute.*

BLUEBERRY AND ORANGE PUDDING WITH BLUEBERRY SAUCE

Serves 6—8

1 egg
½ cup sugar
½ cup milk
1¼ cups self-raising flour
60 g butter, melted
1½ teaspoons grated orange rind
¾ cup fresh or frozen blueberries
cream, ice-cream or yoghurt, to serve

Blueberry Sauce
2 teaspoons cornflour
2 cups fresh or frozen blueberries
1 tablespoon orange juice
1 tablespoon lemon juice
½ cup sugar

Grease a 4-cup capacity metal pudding basin. Line the base of the pudding basin with a circular piece of baking paper to fit in place. Then grease the baking paper with butter or with spray cooking oil.

Whisk the egg and sugar together, then mix in the milk, flour and butter all together. Mix in the orange rind. Fold in the blueberries, then spoon the mixture evenly into the pudding basin. Cover with two layers of foil and tie string around the basin just under the rim to secure the foil and ensure a good seal.

Place pudding basin in cooker, then add boiling water until it reaches two-thirds of the way up the sides of the basin.

Place lid on cooker and cook for 3 hours on High.

To make the blueberry sauce, mix the cornflour with about 1½ tablespoons of cold water to a paste. Place the blueberries, orange and lemon juice and sugar into a small saucepan. Bring to the boil, stirring, then thicken with the cornflour paste.

Remove pudding basin from cooker and leave to stand for 5 minutes. Run a knife around the inside of the basin and invert the pudding onto a plate.

Serve slices of pudding drizzled with ¼ cup or more of the blueberry sauce, plus ice-cream, cream or yoghurt.

Sticky Fig and Date Pudding with Coffee Toffee Sauce

Serves 6

½ cup chopped dried figs, firmly packed
½ cup chopped dates, firmly packed
¾ cup sugar
30 g butter
1 teaspoon bicarbonate of soda
1 egg
1 teaspoon mixed spice
1 cup self-raising flour

Coffee Toffee Sauce
2 teaspoons instant coffee powder or granules
90 g butter
250 g golden syrup
180 g sugar
150 g soft dark brown sugar
¾ cup cream

Grease a 4-cup capacity metal pudding basin. Line the base of the pudding basin with a circular piece of baking paper to fit in place. Then grease the baking paper with butter or with spray cooking oil.

Place the figs, dates, sugar, butter and 1 cup of water in a saucepan and bring to the boil. Simmer for 1 minute. Remove from heat and add the bicarbonate of soda. Stir and leave to cool for 10–15 minutes.

Whisk the egg and add to the mixture along with the mixed spice and flour. Mix well.

Pour into the pudding basin and cover with two layers of foil. Tie string around the basin just under the rim to secure the foil and ensure a good seal.

Place the pudding basin in cooker and pour boiling water until it reaches two-thirds of the way up the outside of the basin.

Place lid on cooker and cook for 4 hours on High.

Meanwhile, to make the coffee toffee sauce, mix the coffee with 3 teaspoons hot water. Place in a medium saucepan with the butter, golden syrup and sugars. Stir over medium heat until the mixture comes to the boil. Simmer, while still stirring, for 5 minutes.

Remove from heat, gradually add the cream and stir well. Return to heat, bring to the boil, stirring, then simmer for 3 minutes more. Allow to cool for a few minutes before serving.

Remove pudding basin from cooker and leave to stand for 5 minutes. Run a knife around the inside of the basin and turn the pudding out onto a serving plate.

Cut the pudding into wedges and place on serving plates. Drizzle the coffee toffee sauce in and around the pudding wedges. For a truly special effect, place drops of cream about 2 cm apart in the sauce, then drag a skewer through them to make tiny hearts.

Note: *Any leftover coffee toffee sauce can be poured into jars and kept in the fridge. Reheat in the microwave, uncovered and in 20-second bursts, for an excellent sauce to serve with ice-cream or pancakes.*

Lemon Marshmallow Meringue Pudding

Serves 6

This delicious recipe has a small, soft crust that perfectly encapsulates the tangy lemon filling. It is topped with a soft marshmallow meringue.

½ cup fresh breadcrumbs
1¼ cups sugar, plus 2 teaspoons extra
⅓ cup cornflour
¾ cup lemon juice
2 teaspoons finely grated lemon rind
4 egg yolks
1 egg
30 g butter

Meringue
4 eggwhites
1 cup sugar
1 teaspoon cornflour

Grease the inside of the slow cooker with a little butter or spray with cooking oil. Mix together the breadcrumbs and 2 teaspoons of sugar and sprinkle over the base and 5 cm up the sides of the cooker.

Mix the cornflour with about ½ cup of cold water to a smooth paste and set aside. Place the lemon juice, lemon rind and 1¼ cups of sugar in a saucepan and bring to the boil. Add the cornflour paste, stirring constantly until thickened, then cook for a further minute, still stirring. Remove from heat and leave to stand for 5 minutes. Whisk in the egg yolks and egg, then the butter. Spoon mixture over the breadcrumb base in the cooker. Turn the cooker setting to Low.

To make the meringue, beat the eggwhites until stiff peaks form, then add the sugar and cornflour and beat until stiff peaks form once more. Spoon over the lemon filling and spread out evenly, making sure it reaches right out to the sides and is slightly lower in the centre. Swirl the mixture with a spatula, knife or fork to form an attractive pattern. Alternatively, the mixture could be piped over the lemon filling.

Place lid on cooker and cook for 2 hours on Low.

Note: *If you have access to a culinary butane torch, you can use it to brown the top a little, but it is by no means necessary.*

STEAMED JAM PUDDING

Serves 6

A steamed jam pudding made in a slow cooker is an interesting thing. The jam is absorbed a little into the pudding and thus flavours the cake component to some extent, while still retaining its characteristic jam layer at the top. To allow for this, a generous amount of jam is used in this recipe.

> 90 g butter, softened
> ½ cup sugar
> 1 egg
> 1½ cups self-raising flour
> ½ cup milk
> ½ teaspoon vanilla essence
> 2½ tablespoons raspberry or other dark jam*
> cream, to serve (optional)

Custard
> 2 cups milk
> ½ cup sugar
> 2 tablespoons cornflour
> 2 egg yolks, whisked

Grease a 4-cup capacity metal pudding basin. Line the base of the pudding basin with a circular piece of baking paper to fit in place. Then grease the baking paper with butter or with spray cooking oil.

Whisk the butter and sugar together, then whisk in the egg until well combined. Fold in the flour, milk and vanilla essence (all at once).

Place the jam in base of pudding basin and spoon the flour mixture over it.

Cover basin with two layers of foil and tie with string around the rim to secure foil and ensure a good seal.

Place pudding basin in cooker and pour boiling water into the cooker until it reaches two-thirds of the way up the sides of basin.

Place lid on cooker and cook for 3½ hours on High.

Remove basin from cooker and leave to stand for 3 minutes, then invert pudding onto a serving plate.

To make the custard, place the milk, sugar and cornflour in a saucepan and bring to the boil, stirring constantly. Cook until thickened. Remove pan from heat and quickly whisk in the egg yolks. Serve slices of pudding with the custard or cream.

Hint: *Use any type of jam or even marmalade as a variation.*

Harlequin Pudding with Raspberry Sauce

Serves 6

This recipe uses raspberry jam in place of red food colouring. If a darker pink is preferred, add about three drops of red food colouring.

  1½ cups self-raising flour
  1¼ cups sugar
  ¾ cup milk
  2 eggs
  125 g butter, melted
  1½ tablespoons cocoa
  1 tablespoon raspberry jam
  1½ cups fresh or frozen raspberries
  ice-cream or sweetened whipped cream, to serve

Grease a 4- or 5-cup capacity metal pudding basin. Line the base of the pudding basin with a circular piece of baking paper to fit in place. Then grease the baking paper with butter or with spray cooking oil.

Place the flour, 1 cup of sugar, ½ cup of milk, eggs and melted butter into a bowl and beat with an electric beater for 2 minutes.

Divide the mixture into three even portions in separate bowls. Combine the cocoa and remaining milk and stir until smooth. Add to one portion and mix well. Add raspberry jam to another portion and mix well.

Place a spoonful of each mixture alternately into the pudding basin to make a pretty pattern (but do not swirl together). Cover the basin with two layers of foil and tie string around the basin just under the rim to secure the foil and ensure a good seal.

Place pudding basin in cooker and pour boiling water into the cooker until it reaches two-thirds of the way up the sides of the basin.

Place lid on cooker and cook for 3 hours on High.

Remove basin from the cooker and leave to stand for 5 minutes. Run a knife around the inside of the basin and invert the pudding onto a plate. Remove baking paper.

Place the raspberries in a small saucepan with 3 tablespoons of water and bring to the boil. Simmer for 5 minutes. Strain if desired. Add the remaining sugar, bring to the boil and cook for a further minute.

Serve slices of pudding with a little raspberry sauce and ice-cream or sweetened whipped cream.

PUMPKIN PUDDING WITH LEMON CREAM

Serves 6

This recipe is a variation of a pumpkin cake that was handed down to me by my grandmother. When she was young her family owned a bakery in Sandy Bay, and this cake was one of their regular products. Its flavour is truly delicious, and is one of the only things containing pumpkin that my young children would ever knowingly eat.

My father lived with us for many years. He had an extreme aversion to pumpkin, however this was his favourite cake. Mind you, we never did tell him about pumpkin being one of its major components. One day a visiting friend commented, 'You'd never think there was pumpkin in this cake would you?' Dad overheard her and immediately spat out the piece of cake he was chewing. He never touched pumpkin cake again; a true case of mind over matter.

The cake made as this pudding in the slow cooker is even better than when made in the oven. It is so flavoursome that it doesn't need a custard or sauce, but a little lemon cream or ice-cream complements it well.

125 g butter
½ teaspoon lemon essence
½ cup sugar
1 egg

½ cup mashed pumpkin
½ cup self-raising flour
½ cup plain flour
250 g dried mixed fruit

Lemon Cream
200 ml cream
2 teaspoons caster or icing sugar
½ teaspoon finely grated lemon rind
2 teaspoons lemon juice

Grease a 4-cup capacity metal pudding basin. Line the base of the pudding basin with a circular piece of baking paper to fit in place. Then grease the baking paper with butter or with spray cooking oil.

Cream together the butter, lemon essence and sugar. Add the egg and whisk, then add the mashed pumpkin and whisk again until well combined. Mix in the flours and dried fruit.

Spoon the mixture into the pudding basin and cover with two layers of foil. Tie string around the basin just under the rim to secure the foil and ensure a good seal.

Place pudding basin in cooker and pour boiling water into the cooker until it reaches two-thirds of the way up the sides of the basin.

Place lid on cooker and cook for 2½ hours on High.

Remove basin from cooker and leave to stand for 10 minutes. Run a knife around the inside of the basin and invert pudding onto a plate.

To make the lemon cream, whisk together the cream and caster or icing sugar until soft peaks form. Fold in the lemon rind and juice. Serve slices of pudding with a little lemon cream.

CARAMEL APPLE STRUDEL ROLL

Serves 6

90 g butter
1½ cups self-raising flour
1 teaspoon lemon juice
½ cup water

Apple Filling
3 apples
½ cup sultanas
¼ cup sugar
1 teaspoon finely grated lemon rind
½ teaspoon ground cinnamon

Caramel Sauce
1½ cups brown sugar
90 g butter
2 tablespoons lemon juice
1 cup water

Grease the inside of the slow cooker with a little butter or spray with cooking oil.

To make the pastry, cut the butter into small dice and rub into the flour with a pinch of salt until mixture resembles breadcrumbs. Make a well in the centre and add the lemon juice and half the water. Gradually work into the flour mixture with a metal spoon, adding extra water, if necessary, to make a soft dough. Set aside.

To make the filling, core and coarsely grate the apples and combine with the sultanas, sugar, lemon rind and cinnamon.

Turn the dough out onto a lightly floured board and roll out to a rectangle, approximately 30 cm x 20 cm.

Spread over the pastry, leaving a 1 cm strip clear around the edge. Brush one half of the edge with a little water. Roll up from the long edge, seal the ends and place in the cooker.

To make the caramel sauce, combine all ingredients in a small saucepan. Bring to the boil and pour over the apple strudel roll.

Place lid on cooker and cook on High for 2–2½ hours.

APPLE GOLDEN SYRUP DUMPLINGS

Serves 4

1 tablespoon butter
½ cup sugar
2 tablespoons golden syrup
cream, ice-cream or yoghurt, to serve

Dumplings
1 cup self-raising flour
3 level teaspoons butter
2 tablespoons coarsely grated apple
milk, to combine

Place butter, sugar, golden syrup and 1½ cups of water in the slow cooker. Place lid on cooker and cook for approximately 40 minutes on High or until boiling.*

When syrup is almost boiling, make the dumplings.

Place the flour in a bowl and rub in the butter with your fingertips. Stir in the grated apple, then mix to a soft dough with milk. Roll into walnut-size balls.

Take a sheet of baking paper slightly larger than the cooker and spray one side with cooking spray or grease with a little butter.

When the syrup is boiling, place dumplings in the syrup. Place baking paper greased-side down on top of cooker and replace lid.

Cook for 25 minutes on High.

Serve with cream, ice-cream or yoghurt.

Hint: *Alternatively, preheat the slow cooker on High. Put the water, butter, sugar and golden syrup in a saucepan and bring to the boil, then pour the syrup mixture into the cooker. Place lid on cooker while you prepare the dumplings.*

APPLE DUMPLINGS IN BUTTERSCOTCH SAUCE

Serves 4

2 apples
1 cup self-raising flour
1 teaspoon sugar
3 teaspoons butter
1 teaspoon finely grated lemon rind
1 egg yolk
1 cup brown sugar, lightly packed
1 tablespoon butter
1 tablespoon golden syrup
ice-cream, cream or yoghurt, to serve

Peel and core the apples and cut into quarters, lengthways. Lightly grease the inside of the slow cooker with butter or spray with cooking oil.

Mix the flour, sugar and a pinch of salt in a bowl. Cut the butter into small pieces and rub into the flour mixture with your fingertips until the mixture resembles fine breadcrumbs. Mix in the lemon rind. Lightly whisk the egg yolk and mix in with about ¼ cup of cold water, or just enough to make a soft dough.

Divide the dough into eight equal pieces and flatten each of them out a little. Take each piece of apple and mould a piece of dough around it. Place the 'dumplings' in the slow cooker.

Place the brown sugar, butter, golden syrup and 1½ cups of water in a small saucepan and bring to the boil. Pour over the dumplings.

Place lid on cooker and cook for 1–1½ hours on High.

Serve dumplings with ice-cream, cream or yoghurt.

POACHED QUINCES WITH CINNAMON SPICE DUMPLINGS

Serves 4

1.2 kg quinces (approximately)
¾ cup sugar
1 cup self-raising flour
2 teaspoons icing sugar
30 g butter
½ teaspoon ground cinnamon
½ teaspoon ground mixed spice
¼ teaspoon ground ginger
2 teaspoons lemon juice
½ cup milk

Peel the quinces, cut into quarters and remove the inner cores. Cut each quarter in half and place in the slow cooker, together with the sugar and ½ cup of water. Stir to combine.

Place lid on cooker and cook overnight or for about 8 hours on Low, by which time the quince will have turned a deep scarlet colour.

Turn cooker setting to High while making the dumplings.

Place the flour, icing sugar and butter into a bowl (it is best to cut the butter into small pieces), then rub together with your fingertips until the mixture resembles breadcrumbs. Mix in the cinnamon, mixed spice and ginger. Make a well in the centre and add the lemon juice and half the milk. Mix them into the dry ingredients, adding more of the remaining milk as necessary to make a soft dough. Roll into walnut-size balls.

Take a sheet of baking paper slightly larger than the slow cooker and spray one side with cooking oil spray or grease with a little butter.

Place the dumplings on top of the quince, cover with the baking paper greased-side down and replace lid. Cook for 45 minutes on High.

Note: *If you wash the quinces first and wipe off the brown powdery 'bloom', you can use the peel and cores to make a beautiful quince jelly, using the recipe on page 232, making adjustments according to the weight of the peel and cores you have on hand.*

MOIST APPLE AND SULTANA DESSERT CAKE

Serves 6

1 egg
½ cup sugar
1 cup self-raising flour
125 g butter, melted
cream, ice-cream or yoghurt, to serve

Apple and Sultana Filling

1 cup grated apple
¼ cup sultanas
½ teaspoon ground cinnamon
¼ teaspoon ground nutmeg
2 teaspoons cornflour
1½ tablespoons lemon juice
½ teaspoon grated lemon rind
1 tablespoon sugar

Topping

2 teaspoons melted butter
1½ teaspoons sugar
½ teaspoon ground cinnamon

Turn cooker setting to High to preheat for 10 minutes.

Grease a 16-cm (or just slightly larger) round cake tin with butter or with spray cooking oil. Line the base of the tin with a circular piece of baking paper to fit in place. Then grease the baking paper with butter or with spray cooking oil.

To make the shortcake, whisk the egg and sugar together, then add the flour and melted butter and mix well.

Spread two-thirds of the shortcake mixture over the base and 1 cm up the sides of the cake tin.

Mix together the apple, sultanas, cinnamon, nutmeg, cornflour, lemon juice, lemon rind and sugar. Spoon over the shortcake mixture in the tin.

Press spoonfuls of the remaining shortcake mixture into discs (just in your hands will do) and place over the apple mixture so that it covers it as much as possible.

Cover the cake tin with foil and tie a piece of string around the rim to ensure a good seal. Place cake tin in the slow cooker. Pour boiling water into the cooker to come 1 cm up the sides of the cake tin.

Place lid on cooker and cook for 4 hours on High.

Remove foil from cake tin and leave to stand for 5 minutes. Invert cake onto a wire rack and leave upside down. Transfer to serving plate when cool.

For the topping, brush cake with the melted butter, then sprinkle with the sugar and cinnamon. Serve warm with cream, ice-cream or yoghurt.

In *A Year in a Bottle*, Sally Wise brings together a mouthwatering collection of more than 100 of her favourite recipes for preserves and conserves. Here are just a few for you to try...

QUINCE JELLY

Makes approximately 1.75 litres

As a stand-alone product Quince Jelly is wonderful on toast or scones or as a topping for a steamed pudding.

> 1.5 kg quinces, washed and chopped
> juice of 1 lemon
> water
> sugar

Combine quinces and lemon juice in a large saucepan and barely cover with water. Bring to the boil and simmer until quinces are tender. Strain through a colander, then strain quince juice through a sieve lined with a double thickness of muslin into a clean saucepan. For each cup of liquid, add 1 cup of sugar. Bring to the boil, stirring occasionally to dissolve sugar, and continue to boil until setting point is reached.

Pour into warm sterilised jars and seal immediately. The jelly can be eaten at once.

TOMATO SAUCE

Makes approximately 7 litres

6 kg tomatoes, roughly chopped
1 kg onions, roughly chopped
750 g sugar
2 cups white or cider vinegar
120 g cooking salt
1½ tablespoons whole cloves
1½ tablespoons allspice berries
½ teaspoon cayenne pepper

Place all ingredients in a large saucepan. Bring to the boil and cook, stirring regularly, for 4 hours. Strain mixture through a sieve, colander or food mill and return to clean saucepan. Bring to the boil and cook for 5 minutes.

Pour into warm sterilised bottles and seal immediately. Invert bottles briefly. Consume at once or store in a cool, dry and dark place for up to 2 years.

Note: *Ground spices may be used instead of the whole spices in this recipe. Bear in mind that these will make the sauce a little darker in colour.*

APRICOT JAM

—⊂○

Makes approximately 1.5 kg

The classic product! Peaches, nectarines or peacharines can be substituted for the apricots.

    1.5 kg halved and stoned apricots, chopped
    juice of 2 lemons
    ¾ cup water
    1.5 kg sugar

Grease a large saucepan with butter. Add apricots, lemon juice and water and stew over medium heat until apricots are soft. Add sugar and bring to the boil, stirring frequently. Continue to boil until setting point is reached, stirring frequently or jam will catch.

Pour into warm sterilised jars and seal immediately. The jam may be eaten as soon as it cools. Store for up to 12 months in a cool, dry and dark place. Refrigerate after opening.

Note: Apricots are inclined to stick and burn when making jams and the like. Greasing the base of the pan with butter before adding the ingredients will help prevent this. I was recently told by a friend that greasing a fork or two and placing them in the mixture while cooking will also help — it's worth a try!

PLUM WORCESTERSHIRE SAUCE

Makes approximately 3 litres

My grandfather used to add a splash of this sauce to my Nan's excellent lamb and vegetable soup at serving time. I also add it to any lamb or beef stew or casserole while they are cooking.

- 1.5 kg damson plums
- 20 cups malt vinegar
- 125 g garlic, peeled
- 125 g salt
- 4 cups treacle
- 750 g brown sugar
- 125 g fresh ginger, bruised
- 60 g cloves
- 30 g allspice berries
- 1 teaspoon cayenne pepper

Combine all ingredients in a large saucepan and bring to the boil. Continue to boil for 3 hours or until lightly thickened.

Strain, pour into warm sterilised bottles and seal. The sauce is ready to eat in 1 month. Store in a cool, dry and dark place for up to 2 years.

REDCURRANT JELLY

Makes approximately 1.25 litres

Try serving turkey with this jelly instead of cranberry sauce. It is also delicious served with duck and ham.

    1.5 kg redcurrants
    water
    sugar

Place redcurrants in a large saucepan and barely cover with water. Bring to the boil and cook for 20 minutes, squashing fruit with a potato masher from time to time. Strain through a colander, then strain resulting liquid through a sieve lined with a double thickness of muslin into a clean saucepan. For each cup of liquid, add 1 cup of sugar. Bring to the boil and cook until setting point is achieved.

Pour into warm sterilised jars and seal immediately. The jelly can be used at once.

ACKNOWLEDGEMENTS

My special thanks to Chris Wisbey, whose shared passion for food and his accompanying sense of fun have contributed greatly to *Slow Cooker* and *A Year in a Bottle* coming into existence.

Many thanks to the people at ABC Hobart, to the helpful test tasters among their number on the mornings of the 'Jams and Preserves' talkback segment.

ABOUT THE AUTHOR

Sally Wise is a regular guest on ABC Local Radio 936 Hobart and writes for *Gardening Australia* and *Green Living* magazines. She runs cooking courses and often demonstrates cookery to community groups and at events such as Gardening Australia Expos. Her previous book was the bestselling *A Year in a Bottle*.

INDEX